CHURCH
FINANCES
FOR PEOPLE WHO
COUNT

CHURCH FINANCES
FOR PEOPLE WHO
COUNT

A basic handbook for Church treasurers, trustees, deacons and ministry staff.

MACK TENNYSON

Zondervan*PublishingHouse*
Academic and Professional Books
Grand Rapids, Michigan

A Division of HarperCollinsPublishers

CHURCH FINANCES FOR PEOPLE WHO COUNT
Copyright © 1990 by Mack Tennyson

Requests for information should be addressed to:
Zondervan Publishing House
Academic and Professional Books
1415 Lake Drive S.E.
Grand Rapids, Michigan 49506

Library of Congress Cataloging in Publication Data

Tennyson, Mack.
    Church finances for people who count : a basic handbook for church
treasurers, trustees, deacons, and ministry staff / Mack Tennyson.
        p.   cm.
    ISBN 0-310-43771-7
    1. Church finance. I. Title.
BV770.T46   1990   90-39729
254.8—dc20   CIP

Edited by Laura Weller
Designed by Louise Bauer

Printed in the United States of America

90 91 92 93 94 95 / PP / 10 9 8 7 6 5 4 3 2 1

To Dianne,
whom I love very much

CONTENTS

ACKNOWLEDGMENTS   **9**
  1. Church Finances and God   **11**
  2. A High Calling: A Spiritual Look at
     Church Treasurers   **24**
  3. A Matter of Common Sense:
     Internal Control   **31**
  4. Learning the Ropes: A Look at
     Record Keeping   **37**
  5. A Never-ending Maze: Taxes   **49**
  6. Ask and It Shall Be Given: Property Gifts   **60**
  7. Counting the Cost: Budgets 101   **70**
  8. More Cost Counting: Budgets 102   **80**
  9. A Spiritual Journey: Finances and
     Building a Church   **91**
 10. Survival: A Church Building Program   **104**
 11. Ox Muzzling: Workers and Pay   **116**
 12. Computers: A Necessary Evil?   **129**

CONCLUSION   **139**

APPENDIX 1. Internal Control Checklist   **141**

APPENDIX 2. Bank Reconciliations   **143**

APPENDIX 3. Sample Budget   **150**

APPENDIX 4. Tax Forms   **154**

ACKNOWLEDGMENTS

Many thanks to these church leaders and colleagues who helped me with this book: Steve Adessa, Bo Beadles, Randy Blyth, Cathy Morris, and Hazel Watson.

1 | *CHURCH FINANCES AND GOD*

Eleven P.M. Pastor Jim turns onto Elm Street—home at last! What a day: a men's prayer breakfast, hospital visits, a Boy Scout meeting, a visit with a wayward member, six calls about church insurance, a sour visit with Brother Ebenezer, a teens spaghetti dinner, and a budget meeting.

Mostly Pastor Jim wants sleep. But he knows his wife wants to talk. After all, she stayed home all day tending the kids. Well, she did get out for a while; she carried the dirty clothes to the laundromat because the washing machine is broken again. Jim is sure he can fix it if he can just get to it.

Sure enough, Jim cannot go to bed until he and Janet tell each other about their day. Janet complains a little about the washing machine, and Jim gets in a few shots about Brother Ebenezer. They pray and crawl into bed. Soon Jim hears Janet's light, sound-asleep breathing.

Thirty minutes later Jim is still lying there staring at the shadow the street light cast on the ceiling. He hears his young son mumbling in his sleep and a dog barking down the street. Jim is wide awake.

Two hours go by. Jim cannot sleep. His mind races the way minds do at two A.M.: "Did I handle Brother Ebenezer the way Jesus would?" "I wish that I had not told that joke about Jello at the teen dinner. It wasn't all that dirty, but it just wasn't right." "I can't believe that budget meeting: three hours of speeches about all sorts of things, and we ended up keeping this year's budget the same for next year."

Finally his thoughts focus. "It is wrong to keep the same budget. You would think that since I am new here something would change because of my goals and my plans." Then an idea grows. It is distant at first, but finally it splashes him in the face like cold water: "I don't have any goals or plans! Sure, I know why I am here: to spread the Gospel and to serve God's people. But I don't have a plan to do it. I have been so mixed up in day-to-day details that I have just been running in circles. This church needs direction. Where is it going, and why is it going there? How can it organize around the goals? How can we point the budget at the goals?"

What an idea! What a release!

Soon the dog stops barking. Jim unsets the alarm, and God allows him to sleep. God felt bad about keeping Jim up; but with Jim so busy, it was the only way he could get a word in edgewise.

CHURCH FINANCES AND SCRIPTURE

It would be nice if we could look in the Bible and find a guide to running church finances, perhaps a beatitude that said something like, "Blessed are the treasurers, for they shall see God." In some respects the Bible is silent on church finances. It does not talk about budgets, finance committees, or financial reports. However, the Bible is not as silent on church finances as it may seem. It outlines a support system through tithes and offerings (Mal. 3:6–12); develops a financial decision-making system through its overseers, deacons, elders, and councils (see, e.g., Acts 6:1–7; 15:1–19); and talks about a corrupt church treasurer (John 12:4–6).

The Bible also talks to church members about spending their money (e.g., caring for the poor and supporting pastors). This counsel applies to churches as well. If a member must care for the poor, how much more should the church use its money for the poor?

Jesus' parable of the talents (Matt. 25:14–30) relates to church finances. You will recall that the departing master gave each of three servants some money which he expected them to invest and give an accounting for when he returned. The first two servants doubled their money, but the third servant buried his in a hole. The master called him a wicked, lazy servant for doing so.

Many people wrongly use this parable, saying that God gives everyone inborn gifts and, in turn, everyone gives God an account of what he or she does with them. This is a good lesson, but it is not the parable's main lesson.

A "talent" in Jesus' day was a unit of money; it did not mean an inborn gift. Over the years people have applied the parable to inborn gifts so much that today we use the word "talents" to mean just that.

If the parable's main lesson is not about inborn gifts, then what is its point? It provides a lesson for both the church and its members on handling money.

First, the parable shows the master as the source of the money. Churches can get into such a tailspin of bazaars, fund-raisers, and special offerings that they forget God is the source. Some pastors advise members to give in faith, saying, "The Lord will provide," yet they worry themselves sick about the church budget. The Bible promises care for God's children, so how much more do the promises apply to God's church?

Second, the parable teaches that hoarding money is a sin. The wicked servant did not run off with the money, nor did he waste it in sin. All he did was fail to use it to advance the master's kingdom. The church treasury is not a place to build wealth. It is simply a pipeline through which God funnels his wealth to care for the poor, advance his Gospel, and otherwise tend to his church.

Third, the parable teaches about a coming judgment, a great heavenly accounting. During this accounting, all people will report on what they did with the money they were given. With Christ we can go before "the throne of grace with confidence" (Heb. 4:16).

OUT OF THE PULPIT

These lessons sound good, but how do we take such high-sounding ideals and use them in our churches? What is the best financial system for churches? Each church must choose a financial system that fits its needs: it must decide how the money decisions are made; who approves expenses; who prepares the budget; who handles investments; and who prepares the financial reports, receipts, and checks. The list goes on and on. How does one design a church financial system that works?

Unfortunately, there is no one system that is right for every church. The financial system you set for your church depends on your church and on you. The financial system for a 2000-member church is not like the system for a 200-member church or a 20-member church.

Churches have distinct natures. In some churches, members want to take part in every decision. These churches need a financial system that allows for input from the members. Others want church leadership to do everything. These churches need a financial system that focuses on the church board.

In addition, different types of pastors need different types of financial systems. Some pastors like stirring around in the church's money decisions; others do not. Some pastors are naive about finances; others have strong financial backgrounds. When designing a system, think about your own situation.

Finally, different church goals help to develop different financial systems. For instance, one church's mission is caring for the poor, so it needs a system that quickly reviews requests for money and makes payments. Another church focuses on outreach, so it needs a system that supports the outreach program. Different sizes, natures, pastors, and missions force churches to tailor financial systems to meet their needs.

UNITY IN CHURCH SYSTEMS

Each church has many systems. It has a financial system, an outreach system, a benevolence system, a personnel system, a building maintenance system, and so forth. In many churches these systems evolve by need. This is not all bad, but it is easy for churches to end up with all sorts of systems, some that help the other systems and some that hurt them.

The financial system is not something merely to be added to the present church system. All systems should be tuned to work together toward the same purpose. They should be analyzed on a regular basis to determine if they still work. The next section on financial systems applies to all church systems, not just finances. Use the guidelines presented there to see if all the systems in your church are working in unity.

DESIGNING A SYSTEM

No matter how big or small a church is, no matter what its nature, and no matter what its mission—every system in it should have these features: planning, organizing, directing, and controlling.

Planning

The trouble in Pastor Jim's church arises from the lack of comprehensive planning. Some people in his church feel that they spend too much time planning: "All we do in this church is have meetings—budget meetings, nominating meetings, board meetings. We are always meeting." Pastor Jim's church has plenty of meetings, but it lacks direction; it needs an overall sense of mission and purpose. Some churches wander about not knowing where they are going. In other churches the mission and purpose pervade every activity. Building mission and purpose truly requires the grace of God. One way to start is to develop a church mission statement.

A dusty mission statement sitting on a shelf is wasteful.

One way to give it life is to use it. Review every program, expense, fund-raising activity, and every other decision in light of the church's mission. Discard everything that does not agree with the mission statement—or else change the mission statement.

Some Christians see planning as wrong. Their idea is that if they hang loose, sooner or later the Holy Spirit will show them what to do. Such believers' fruit shows their error.

The Bible teaches planning: David wanted to build God's temple, but God would not allow him to, so he spent his last years gathering building materials. The planning was so precise that the workers took the materials to the site ready to erect without tools. "In building the temple, only blocks dressed at the quarry were used, and no hammer, chisel or any other iron tool was heard at the temple site while it was being built" (1 Kings 6:7).

When you are planning, build on your church's strengths, not its weaknesses. Just as different people have different spiritual gifts, so also different churches have different gifts. For instance, Brother Bill is good at making repairs, but he would be a poor church treasurer. So also, Smyrna Baptist cares for the poors' needs, Ephesus Bible Church has a strong bus program, Sardis Christian Church focuses on older people, and Berea has a strong youth ministry. Churches have spiritual gifts much like people.

Some churches do not do anything well because they try to do everything. Do not let your planning sessions digress too far into what the church ought to be doing but is not. When you are looking at the church's mission, focus on the church's strong points and perhaps add one or two new programs.

Many mission statements read like the Great Commission: ". . . to spread the Gospel to the people of Summerville and the world." There is nothing wrong with that. However, sooner or later the high-sounding mission statement must be broken down into workable goals, such as, "This year the church will hold two evangelistic meetings," and strategies, such as "We will form an outreach committee that will be allotted 10 percent of the church's income."

Goals can be stated either in action terms or in result terms. Churches should state their goals in action terms. A business may state its goal in result terms, for example, "During the next year we will increase sales by 15 percent." But a church would be leaving God out of the picture if it stated, "We will increase our membership by 15 percent," because more than work is needed to gain new members. The apostle Paul writes that we are to work, but the results are God's: "I planted the seed, Apollos watered it, but God made it grow" (1 Cor. 3:6).

Christian work is good in itself, so state your goals in action terms: "We will hand out five hundred Bibles." "We will visit every nonattending church member." "The youth department will hold twelve youth outings this year." Focus on activity, not results.

After you set your goals, every expense, equipment purchase, fund-raising project, and everything else the church does with money should spring from the church's mission statement, goals, and strategies.

After your church has found its mission, set its goals, and made plans for reaching those goals, it is ready for the next step: organizing.

Organizing

A church's structure is the way it works on its goals. Saying that one structure is right for every church would be the same as saying that every church has the same goals. Church structures are as varied as goals.

Churches should divide into segments. They are parts of the structure that do certain things or serve certain groups. Dividing into segments will do five things for your church: (1) Make supervision easier. Dealing with a Sunday school director is easier than dealing with every teacher; (2) give the segment leader good leadership training. As leaders excel in less-important segments (e.g., the flower committee), they may grow into leaders of more complex segments, (e.g, the Sunday school). Some pastors see their job as almost all leadership training; (3) give members belonging and fulfillment. Churches can be so large that members do not feel like members. They feel as if they cannot give anything to such a large group. Segments give members a chance to feel like they belong and can truly help; (4) provide a basis for rating programs. For instance, analysis of the youth department provides a good starting point in determining how well the overall church is serving its youth; and (5) give the church a broader basis for decision making. With segments, all the decisions are not made at the top. For instance, the church board may decide the year's flower budget, but a flower committee decides what flowers to buy. Or the board may allocate a certain amount of money for the youth department, but, the youth department decides what programs to have. These five points hold true whether a church divides into segments by function or by programs.

Most churches organize by function: Sunday school, youth groups, women's and men's groups, outreach groups, music department, community services, church maintenance, and so on. This makes sense. The jobs are clearly defined, and the people involved know what to do.

As churches grow, function-based structures start showing their weaknesses. For example, the Sunday school teen leader may plan a picnic on the same day as the youth leader. Or the youth group may want to do a special song for the church service, but the choir leader does not know about it. The larger the church, the more these problems occur.

To deal with such problems, some churches organize around the people it serves. This is called a program structure. For instance, the youth program's team includes the youth leader, the youth Sunday school teacher, and the youth choir leader, etc. They devise the plans for the youth. A similar structure is used for each age group.

An outreach program can be set up the same way. The outreach committee selects the church's outreach projects. The Sunday school director, the youth leader, the choir leader, etc., work on this committee, leading the church's outreach.

The program structure also has problems. People may not be used to working in program teams. Also jobs are not as clearly defined as in function-type structures, and dividing church activities into programs is difficult. Questions may arise, such as: Who pays for church organ repairs? Who decides which class uses which Sunday school classroom? If you divide the budget by programs, which program pays the power bill, or how do you parcel it to the programs?

A church's structure affects the way it handles its finances. The way the budget, financial reports, and purchases are done depends on the church's structure. For instance, if a church has a function-based structure, it prepares its budget and reports its expenses by function. Function heads approve the expenses for their functions. If a church organizes around programs, it prepares its budget and reports its expenses by program. Program heads approve the expenses for their programs. So when you are setting up your church's structure, think about handling the finances.

Directing

Directing is the most difficult part of any system. It has two aspects: directing the people involved in the system and directing the system as a whole.

Directing People. Books on managing church workers say something like, "The workers are volunteers, so do not treat them like employees." Today even companies are realizing that they must not treat their employees like employees. Good management says that employers should get workers to buy into the company's goals. The best workers are those who work hard because they believe in what the company is doing. Companies build this loyalty into their workers by involving them in company goal setting and planning and by allowing them a share in the success.

If teamwork is valuable for companies, it is even more

valuable for churches. This is obvious in areas such as youth work and outreach. Youth leaders will work harder if they feel they are team members rather than doing things only because it is their job.

Teamwork is especially important in the area of church finances. Many open, warm church leaders turn into Mr. Hydes when it comes to finances because (1) there may be misunderstandings due to lack of information about finances, (2) the state of church finances may seem overwhelmingly troublesome, and (3) they may have the mistaken notion that the area of finances is purely logical.

These three causes are all the more reason to nurture strong teamwork in finances. Since there may be misunderstandings due to lack of information about church finances, there is need for open communication among the pastor, treasurer, and the finance committee.

Because church finances may be in a mess, everyone involved must work as a team. There once was a church treasurer who saw a disaster coming but did not shout a warning or ease its extent. When asked why she did nothing, she said, "The pastor was calling the shots; I just did what I was told." If the treasurer had felt like she was a team member, things would have turned out differently.

Church finances are not any more logical than other church systems. Only by the Holy Spirit's blessings can our decisions find the right path. Searching for God's will for the finances of a church is a team effort, just as it is for the other systems in the church.

Directing the System. Besides directing the people in the system, someone must direct the system. Someone must ensure that the steps outlined here keep working. Once people become involved in the busyness of church work, it is easy for them to forget that they are working by a plan that is organized to achieve certain goals and that needs direction and evaluation. It is important to step back from the bustle and review what one is doing and why.

Controlling

Controlling is the last step in managing. It is comparing the system's outcome to the system's goals. Are you doing what you set out to do? This is the feedback link that helps you to determine if your strategies, structure, and directing are allowing you to meet your goals.

Some churches float from program to program without evaluating their programs. There are three reasons for this. The first is that they feel they must maintain an upbeat Christian outlook. From their viewpoint, saying something negative about a program would only bring harm. But this is no excuse for failing to review programs.

The second reason is the ubiquitous Brother Ebenezers who see all programs as failures. Even if we ignore their comments, they hurt the review process by making honest members afraid to do honest program reviews because they fear they will look like Brother Ebenezer.

The third reason churches avoid evaluating their programs is because it is difficult. In business, evaluation is simpler. We ask such questions as: "What was the return on your investment?" "What does it cost per unit?" and "Which is cheaper?" Since money is a major focus in running a business, it gives an easy basis for reviewing programs.

But churches are in the soul business, and that makes it more difficult to evaluate programs. Suppose an outreach program cost a billion dollars and only one person received eternal life. That is a good deal. God's Son died on the cross for one person. A billion dollars is a small price for us to pay. However, the money may be more useful elsewhere. A program where two people receive eternal life would be better, and a program where three are redeemed is even better.

Evaluating programs does not keep the Holy Spirit from guiding us. It may be one way the Spirit works: Pastor Jim once woke with a great idea. He was sure that the Spirit had led him to it. There are three tax experts in his church. He convinced them to put on a tax seminar as an outreach tool. This would be a real community service and a way to meet people. They set up a full program and advertised it, but nobody came except the pastor and the three tax experts.

Was Jim wrong in his view of the Spirit's guiding? It could have been the pizza he ate before going to bed. Or it could have been one of those weird brainstorms that people have during the night. He would not have been the first Christian to make such a mistake. But it also could have been the Holy Spirit. God could have had any of a number of reasons for wanting Jim to go through such an experience. However, Jim would have been foolish to insist on having tax seminars over and over again.

All programs should include a plan for evaluation in light of its goals.

Summary

The church's financial program should include all the basic parts of good management: planning, organizing, directing, and controlling. Figure 1.1 gives a sample financial system for the Summerville Community Church. How will you set up a financial system for your church?

Fig. 1.1. A financial system for Summerville Community Church

Planning   During the next year the church will:
    1. Visit the members about their stewardship.
    2. Prepare timely financial reports and budgets.
    3. Set up an internal control system over the money.

Organization 1. A finance committee will be set up to supervise budgeting, cash payments, and other church finances. It will consist of the pastor, the treasurer, and two others appointed by the church board. It will meet monthly.
    2. A stewardship committee will be set up to inspire stewardship. It will consist of the stewardship leader, the treasurer, and two others appointed by the church board. It will meet quarterly.

Directing   During the year the pastor and other church leaders will look after the process.

Control   At year end, the finance and stewardship committees will prepare reports. The church board will review the goals and look over the documents to ensure that the church is moving toward its goals.

2 | A HIGH CALLING: A SPIRITUAL LOOK AT CHURCH TREASURERS

It is Sunday morning, and Pastor Jim is in rare form during his sermon. Listen to him: "Think of an eye. No, not an eye built into a face—think of an eye sitting off by itself. It is yucky looking but harmless. It cannot do anything. It just sits there looking around. Since it does not have arms or a mouth, it cannot react to what it sees. Of course, some may argue that it cannot see at all without a brain to process the image. It cannot run. It cannot talk. It cannot do anything at all, sitting there by itself."

Brother Ebenezer just rolls his eyes and looks at his watch. Pastor Jim is not his favorite speaker.

But Paul used the same image: "If the whole body were an eye, where would the sense of hearing be? If the whole body were an ear, where would the sense of smell be?" (1 Cor. 12:17). Paul's point is that all gifts are equally needed. We must have various gifts in the church before any single gift is useful. A church where everyone is a healer is useless—who do they heal? A church with all teachers is chaotic—who do they teach? What good is a prophet in a church filled with prophets? Have you ever tried to tell the future to someone who already knows it?

"There are different kinds of service, but the same Lord. There are different kinds of working, but the same God works all of them in all men" (1 Cor. 12:5–6). This is good news for church treasurers. Of all the jobs in the church, theirs is the hardest to fake. They can trust God to give them the skill to do their job.

When we think about the gifts of the Spirit we usually think of tongues, preaching, or prophecy; but Paul, in his list of the Spirit's gifts in 1 Corinthians 12:28, names "administration" as a gift. Caring for finances is a time-consuming part of administration, so when Paul talks about the gift of administration, he has, among others, church treasurers in mind.

The treasurer's job is vital; the whole church collapses if no one does it. If no one pays the preachers, they may stop preaching. If no one pays the electric bill, the power will be shut off. If no one pays the mortgage, the buildings will be lost. Giving money to God is a Christian's duty, and someone must receive it for God. Hence the treasurer is very valuable.

You who are treasurers may ask, "What if I don't have this gift? What if God didn't call me to be a treasurer?" Perhaps you do not have the gift of administration. Take an honest look at your life. Certain traits suggest that you have this gift: Do you like to keep things neat and orderly? Are you thorough? Are you patient? Do you have a quiet tongue? Do you sense God's power over money?

If you have these traits, you likely have the gift of administration. However, if you are missing one or two, God may be planning to give them to you. The above verses say that God will give you the skills you need. It may be that God wants you to be a treasurer so that he can develop these traits in your life.

Notice that these traits mention nothing about any previous background in managing and accounting for money. Traits such as patience and thoroughness are much more needed than financial experience. A church choosing a treasurer should get someone with these traits rather than, say, a CPA without them. If you do not have these traits *and* do not desire to develop them, you have some other gift rather than the gift of administration.

Before you write yourself off, you need to find someone else to do the job. According to the body images drawn by Paul, someone in the church has the gift. If not, rethink your decision. God may want to develop this gift in you.

The necessary traits of a treasurer are listed in detail below.

NEATNESS AND ORGANIZATION

Are you neat and orderly? Look at your own records. Do you know where things are when you need them? Do you put things where they belong at home, or do you just stuff them anywhere? It pleases many people to learn that the word *neat* never appears in the Bible. But order and neatness are essential for keeping church records. Ask the church to buy you the tools you need for this job: file cabinets, folders, stationery, dividers, etc. I know one treasurer who has devoted a corner of her house to this ministry. She has two small desks, one for her work and the other solely for church records.

THOROUGHNESS

Do you finish jobs that you start? Do you cut corners when the going is rough? Thoroughness is neatness and order in action. Usually one finds both of these character traits together in a person. The Bible contains thoughts on thoroughness: "Whatever your hand finds to do, do it with all your might" (Eccl. 9:10), and "Do you see a man skilled in his work? He will serve before kings; he will not serve before obscure men" (Prov. 22:29). People who have the gift of administration face tasks with diligence, and do not look for ways to cut corners. They are skillful, careful, and complete about everything they do.

It is easy to see how vital thoroughness is. Sloppy, haphazard methods can destroy a church in just a few months. A casual treasurer has partial records, unpaid bills, and undeposited receipts. A good one is careful with the records, money, and other aspects of the job.

The treasurer's job is one of the few posts in the church

that requires work fifty-two weeks of the year. Treasurers need vacations, but they must find someone to fill in while they are away. Many officers in the church can be away for a few weeks, and the church will not miss them. But if the treasurer disappears for a few weeks, the church is hurt.

PATIENCE

All jobs in the church body require patience. Pastors wait for the harvest of their labors. Teachers wait until heaven to learn of their impact. Likewise, it may take years for the fruits of a good treasurer's labors to show. This is especially true in churches where there is a history of money problems.

Treasurers also need patience in dealing with church members. The sweetest people in the church may become vicious when they start dealing with money.

QUIET TONGUE

A flapping tongue can destroy anyone's ministry, including a treasurer's. There are two aspects of the job that require a quiet tongue. The first relates to Matthew 6:3–4: "But when you give to the needy, do not let your left hand know what your right hand is doing, so that your giving may be in secret. Then your Father, who sees what is done in secret, will reward you."

Following Christ's teaching is difficult if treasurers reveal the amount people give. How can people give without any thought of what others think if they know the treasurer will reveal it?

The second reason treasurers should never talk about church members' giving relates to people who do not give or who give very little. God is concerned that his followers give with a sacrificial and cheerful heart: "Each man should give what he has decided in his heart to give, not reluctantly or under compulsion, for God loves a cheerful giver" (2 Cor. 9:7). Giving for any other reason is wrong. So church-leaders who, even unintentionally, shame members into giving, destroy God's purpose. Being cheerful about giving is difficult for some people, especially when they are the focus of gossip over giving. In some churches the names of the people who give and the amounts they give are the best kept secrets in the flock.

It is easy to judge. If Brother Jones drives a bright new Cadillac and lives in a big house, we are quick to decide that he should be giving more.

There is danger in such thinking, for we may be wholly wrong in our estimation of a person's giving power. A person could be sending thousands of dollars straight to overseas missions without the church treasurer's knowledge. Thus the treasurers would be wrong to judge that person. God says, "Man looks on the outward appearance, but the Lord looks at the heart" (1 Sam. 16:7).

RECOGNIZES THE POWER OF GOD OVER MONEY

"The silver is mine and the gold is mine, declares the Lord Almighty" (Hag. 2:8). Good treasurers must have a vision of God's power over money. There are at least three reasons for this.

First, if they know the money belongs to God, they will not steal it.

Second, since treasurers serve (officially or unofficially) as stewardship leaders of churches, they must see that God owns all the money. They must practice sacrificial giving before they can encourage and explain the role of giving in the Christian experience, which includes (1) why God wants us to give when he does not need the money, (2) the purpose of the tithe in today's church, (3) the role of special offerings to God, (4) the blessings promised by God to faithful givers, and (5) the gift of the Spirit called giving (see Rom. 12:8).

Churches often appoint stewardship leaders other than the treasurer. This makes sense, because stewardship leaders have a ministry different from that of treasurers. They talk about giving, answer questions on the subject, and encourage personal giving plans. They do not need many of the traits that make good treasurers. However, they need to be outgoing, friendly, and willing to speak up. It is unusual to find someone who has the traits of both a good treasurer and a good stewardship leader, so it makes sense to divide the work into two jobs. However, even if the church has a stewardship leader, the treasurer still needs to know the job's theological basis.

A third and very serious reason good treasurers need to recognize God's ownership over money is that since the money they are taking care of is not theirs, only the church board should say how it is to be spent.

Early in Pastor Jim's ministry, when he was a youth pastor, he found out what can happen if a church treasurer fails to recognize that the money is God's. One night at a church board meeting, the board was deciding whether to buy a video tape recorder and television. Pastor Jim wanted the equipment so he could show videos to the teens. The senior pastor wanted to use it in soul winning. Several laypersons mentioned ways that it would improve their ministries. Most people spoke in favor of the purchase, but a few thought that it was wrong to buy a video tape recorder. The treasurer said, "Movies are the Devil's workshop. They'll start with good movies but gradually they'll go downhill. You mark my words." After heated debate the board voted to get the video recorder.

Several weeks later Pastor Jim planned a program for the teenagers and was going to rent some travelogues for his program. He dropped by the treasurer's house to pick up a check for the video recorder. The treasurer refused to give Jim the check because he still thought that it was wrong to buy a video recorder.

Though this sounds strange, it is very common. The church board may approve something, but the pastor has to jump through hoops to get the money from the treasurer. Treasurers deal with the financial health of the church, carefully accounting for and investing the funds to get the greatest return. Managing the church's funds is exacting and time consuming. It is easy to see why they may soon start to think the money is theirs. Though they would not think of stealing the money, they want complete control. This is wrong, because the money belongs to God. Treasurers are morally and legally bound to carry out church boards' decisions.

If you are a treasurer who has taken too much control over God's money, you need to deal with the problem. Pray that God will change your heart so that it is less focused on things and more aware of people. If you still see a problem after several weeks of diligent prayer, you should gracefully resign.

There is much freedom in knowing that the money belongs to God and not to you and that the money problems of the church belong to God and not to you. The problems of the church fall on the church board, who has total power to spend the money and to deal with the concerns that go with it. Treasurers are only stewards who hold money and spend it according to board decisions.

A good church treasurer (1) sees that the job is a gift of the Spirit, (2) knows that the job is vital to the life of the church, (3) keeps others' giving secret, (4) avoids bias against people because of their giving, (5) knows the job's theological basis, and (6) sees that the money is God's and therefore follows the board's decisions.

3 | A MATTER OF COMMON SENSE: INTERNAL CONTROL

Pastor Jim went to college with a young man named Fred whose main problem was money. Creditors were always at his heels. Fred's lifelong dream was to preach, and after college he accepted the pastorate of a small country church. While moving into the parsonage, Fred broke out in praise: "God is blessing me! I won't have to worry about my creditors now; I'll pay them off. Those Philistines will never bother me again!"

Less than a year later the church fired Fred for stealing offerings.

What went wrong? Did Fred's halo slip? Did the church make a mistake when they hired him? Sin is sin, and there is never an excuse for sin; but the church put Fred in the place that led to his downfall.

As Fred moved out of the parsonage he explained to Pastor Jim: "I made more money than I ever had; I also spent more. What a mess—the worse mess of my whole life! Every week they gave me the offering to give to the treasurer, and I took a little. I planned to pay it back. A member caught me putting money into my pockets. I'm ruined."

Fred accepted full blame for his actions, but good internal control in the church could have prevented such a problem. *Internal control* is accounting jargon. It is a checks and balances system to prevent stealing. Internal control does four things.

First, it makes it difficult for someone to steal the church's money. Some Christians do not like the idea of guarding the church's money. They say: "Why do we need to worry about God's money? He can protect it." This is true. However, God gives us brains and expects us to use common sense. We do not leave the church doors unlocked, and we do not allow just anyone to be church treasurer.

Second, by making stealing difficult, internal control removes useless snares. The church is to be a refuge, not a trap for those who handle the money.

Third, good internal control reduces errors in the records. It forces the treasurer to resolve these errors. It comforts the treasurer to know that things are right.

Finally, good internal control protects the treasurer and others from false charges of stealing.

Internal control is easy. It is simply this: control of assets is kept apart from the record keeping of assets. You see an example of this every time you go to a grocery store. The cash register makes one tape for you and one for management. If the system is run right, the cashier cannot touch the manager's tape. The manager cannot touch the money. At shift's end, the cash in the drawer is compared with the tape. Cashier and manager watch each other.

This is a simple process, but separating the assets from the record keeping brings about the four benefits listed above: (1) It tells the manager whether the cashier is stealing from the store, (2) it keeps the cashier from undue temptation, (3) it aids in record keeping by giving the manager a correct sales record, and (4) it gives the cashier peace to know that the manager cannot make false claims.

In the church setting this process has two parts—internal control over cash receipts and internal control over cash payments.

INTERNAL CONTROL OVER CASH RECEIPTS

A church often gets cash, so a church needs a good system to handle cash. To set up internal control over cash, the church board appoints a treasurer and a helper. The helper controls the cash, and the treasurer keeps the records. The helper is not the assistant treasurer. That is, if the treasurer is absent from church for a time, the church must find someone other than the helper to take over the treasurer's duties. Likewise, the helper must find someone other than the treasurer to take over the helper's duties. This keeps the duties separate.

A good helper is reliable. He or she is often in church and finds a substitute when needed. The helper can add and subtract and can keep a neat checkbook. The helper keeps the church's checkbook, and the treasurer does the bookkeeping.

Fig. 3.1. Internal control of cash receipts for Summerville Community Church

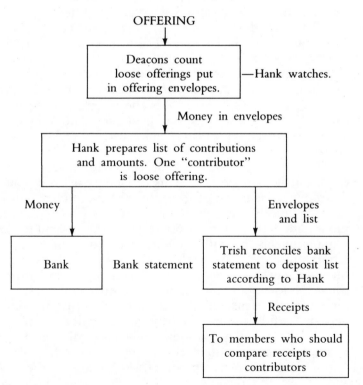

Suppose a church names Trish as church treasurer and Hank as the helper. They process receipts like this: After church service Hank the helper and a deacon take the offering into a back room. They count the loose offerings. They open the envelopes and compare the amount in the envelopes to the amount written on the envelopes. The deacon makes a note of the amount of loose receipts and later gives it to Trish the treasurer. Hank puts the loose offering in an envelope. Later he makes a list of the names of each person who gave and the amount. One name on the list is "loose receipts." He totals the list and makes a deposit slip. Three totals must agree: the list total, the deposit slip total, and the cash and checks total. This process is simple if the helper is careful. Careless counting or incorrectly writing down amounts will cause the totals to differ.

When all three amounts are the same, Hank takes the money to the bank. He gives Trish the donor list and bank receipt, keeping copies for himself. He also gives Trish the offering envelopes, because they tell her which funds to put the money in. Trish checks to make sure the list and the bank receipt agree. She records the receipts, using Hank's list, just as though she received the money. She compares the loose receipts amount from Hank's list to the deacon's note amount.

No one can steal. The deacon watches Hank. Trish never touches any money. Hank is the only one who touches the money. Hank, of course, can take the money and run, but he cannot secretly steal the money. If Hank steals some money and lies about the loose receipts, the amount for loose receipts on his list will differ from the amount the deacon reports to Trish. If Hank steals and lies about what a member gave, the receipt Trish gives to the member will show the lower amount, and the member will question the difference. If Hank tells the truth on the list but does not deposit the full amount, the bank receipt will differ from the list, and Trish will question him when she balances the bank account. A good system covers every angle (fig. 3.1).

If Trish did each step herself, she could steal the money and falsify the records and not get caught. With good internal control, the one who holds the money cannot steal without the records showing it, and the record keeper cannot swindle, because he or she never touches the money.

INTERNAL CONTROL OVER CASH PAYMENTS

Internal control over cash payments is even simpler (fig. 3.2). The first rule for setting up control is that all payments must start with a written request giving the reason for the request, which fund to charge, and whom to pay. These requests are useful later if someone questions a certain payment and the treasurer has forgotten why it was made.

Most claims are bills, such as the electric bill or water bill, but some are requests for money from the pastor or a member. These requests must be made in writing.

For example, if the youth leader wants a check for the money he spent on a teen campout, he must scribble out a note asking for the money and telling what fund to take it from. The treasurer then decides if it is proper.

On a routine basis, say twice a month, Trish lists the people who deserve checks and gives Hank a copy of the list. He also gets the bills. Hank reviews the list and the bills. He ensures that each payment is proper. Whether the board approves the payment is not his worry; he simply looks for suspicious payments by Trish, such as payments for her water bill or checks to her mother.

After his quick review, Hank writes and mails the checks to the people on the list. He jots down the check number on the list and gives it back to Trish.

Trish keeps track of the bank balance. It is her fault if the account is overdrawn. From Trish's point of view, Hank is just writing the checks she would have written anyway.

Trish does not deal with the bank. Hank makes deposits and writes checks. Trish the treasurer is not on the signature card at the bank. Likewise, Hank the helper keeps away from the records. Without a two-person system, Trish could write checks to herself and never be caught. But the two-person system makes it hard for Trish to steal money she does not touch. Since Hank does not touch the records, crooked checks from Hank would show up when Trish balanced the bank account.

Fig. 3.2. Internal control of cash payments
for Summerville Community Church

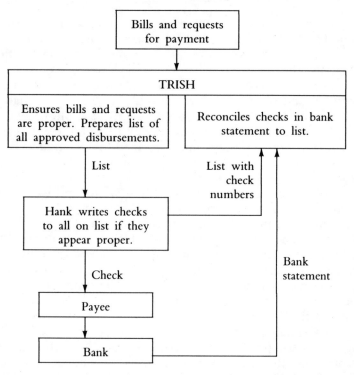

A good internal control system is a central part of proper stewardship over the money that God gives to us. It might have saved Fred, and it avoids countless problems in churches. See appendix 1 for a list of ideal internal control features for churches.

4 | *LEARNING THE ROPES: A LOOK AT RECORD KEEPING*

Two A.M. Pastor Jim is just returning from an out-of-town trip, and he stops by the church to get the papers he needs before tomorrow's board meeting. Driving into the church parking lot, he notices that a second-floor light is on. "Who left the lights on this time?" he mumbles.

Then he sees it. He is not sure at first. "There it is again!" he exclaims silently. "Somebody is moving around in there! Somebody is in there!"

"What room is that anyway?" He counts the windows. He knows the bathroom window because it is smaller than the rest. He counts over to the window with the light on: "It's the church office. There are only three keys to that office!" Jim has one, the secretary has one, and the church treasurer has one.

Jim's mind races with excitement. "The safe is in there. I bet someone is knocking over that safe. Last week's offerings are still in there. What should I do? I'll just go up there. No, that's stupid. I'll call the police."

Fortunately, a patrol car turns the corner onto Elm Street, and Jim flags it down. He shows the policewoman the light and the movement in the church. The policewoman calls for a backup, and Pastor Jim gives her his master key. She then tells Jim that it would be best for him to remain in his car. Another police car arrives. The policewoman and her backup go through the side door.

The minutes tick away. After what seems like an hour,

Jim sees a lot of movement in the room. In a few minutes the policewoman appears at the door with the church treasurer in handcuffs.

Jim quickly explains that this is the church treasurer and that it is okay for him to be in the room. The police take off the handcuffs and leave.

Sam, the treasurer, starts to laugh. He says, "I have never been so scared in my life. I was sitting up there trying to do the bank reconciliation, and I couldn't get it to balance. I was on the verge of tears. Have you ever tried to do something and it wouldn't work; and the harder you worked on it, the worse it got, until you were about to cry? Well that's the way I was. Then I heard this noise out in the hall. It was the sound of someone stumbling and the voice of a female lightly cursing. I was scared silly. All of a sudden a male voice shouted, 'This is the police! Come out with your hands up.' I nearly wet my pants. It never crossed my mind that they were talking to me. I thought they were after the female voice, so I ducked under my desk. In a few minutes they shouted it again. That time I hollered, 'She's not in here officer, she's out there somewhere.' Then the female voice said, 'Who are you talking about?' Well, we stayed there for quite a while and hollered back and forth until the police convinced me that they were after me. That's when we all came down."

Normally a church treasurer does not have such an exciting life. But one thing in the story that most likely will happen to all treasurers is being out of balance and being on the verge of tears. Church record keeping is easy to understand but sometimes hard to do.

This chapter shows the church's basic records and how to keep them. The system shown here is handy for small- and medium-sized churches. Simplicity, ease, and cash control are its major features. If your church has more than one hundred contributors a month or writes more than thirty checks a month, it should consider computer record keeping. But even in a computer system the principles shown here still apply. If you have taken an accounting course and can handle such things as special journals, ledgers, and checkbooks, skip this chapter. Just set up an accounting system using those tools.

FUNDS

A fund, for our purposes, is money that is ready for a specific use within the church. For example, many churches have a building fund, money set aside for the building. Donors may specify that the money they give is only for the building. Also, the church board may approve transfers into it from the general fund. Specific gifts and transfers increase the building fund; checks written for work done reduce the building fund.

Other funds are used in the same manner. For example, the youth work fund is money set aside to pay for youth activities. It comes from specific gifts or transfers from the church general fund. Funds can be set up for such things as soulwinning and telephone expenses.

One fund that all churches have is a general fund. It covers the church's routine expenses, such as electric bills and salaries. Using this fund, the church board also provides more money to other funds (e.g., building and youth work).

Generally a church has only one checking account, but each fund claims some of the money. Suppose that the following funds have these balances:

General fund	$2,000
Building fund	4,000
Youth work	1,000
Poor fund	$500
Total for all funds	$7,500

General fund	Lay outreach fund
Building fund	Retreat fund
Soul-winning fund	Foreign missions fund
Youth work fund	Educational fund
Tithe fund	Church school fund
Community service fund	Vacation Bible school fund

Poor fund	Special programs fund
Van-buying fund	Salaries fund
Flower fund	Grounds fund

Fig. 4.1. Common funds

The checking account balance is $7,500. If the board transfers $500 from the general fund to youth work, the general fund will become $1,500 and the youth work fund will become $1,500. The checking account total will still be $7,500. The funds' total must always equal total cash.

Your church can have as many funds as it wants. Figure 4.1 lists common ones; your own fund list will include only those your church needs. For example, a church that sponsors a Vietnamese refugee family will have a refugee fund. People give directly to the fund, and the church board gives it some general fund money. Then the project leader will know exactly how much to spend.

Each fund is under someone's care. This is one good feature of the fund system. Youth leaders look at the youth work fund and know exactly what they have to run their program, church board members look at the building fund and know exactly what they have for the building, and so forth. Everyone likes this system: the program leaders know exactly how much they have; and the church board can easily move a certain amount to a specific fund, freeing them from dealing with continual requests. This system also frees the treasurer from concern over how much money there is for every program. If the youth leader asks for some money for a teen outing and the fund has the money, he gets it. If not, he must go to the board. Keeping track of how much is set aside for the youth is a simple process for the treasurer.

Some funds that the church treasurer handles belong to other groups. Suppose that your denomination has a foreign mission thrust named The Hudson Taylor Foreign Mission Offering. Once a year the church promotes this offering, and during the year members also give to it. You need a fund that receives the money that comes in and holds it until you send a check to the proper place. If you did not have a fund system, the mission money could easily become mingled with other offerings and perhaps be spent on the electric bill.

JOURNALS

Let us now look at the nuts and bolts of record keeping. First, you need some tools. You need a desk-top adding machine that makes a tape. (A hand-held one is not sufficient; having a tape will help you find errors.) Put your church's name on it and keep it at your house or wherever you do your treasurer's work.

You also need a journal. It is an oversized book with metal pegs binding its hard covers and allowing the user to add or remove pages. Each page *back* has a two- or three-inch-wide column for writing the reason for each entry. The rest of the page has columns for numbers, as does the reverse, or front, side.

Now imagine these pages bound in a book. When you open the book, you see the first page's front. It has nothing but number columns. When you turn the page, things neatly fall together. The first page's back has the column for writing the reason for the entry. Right of that column are many columns for number writing. The columns extend all the way across the entire open book—across the back of the first page to the binding and from the binding all the way across the second page's front. This gives you a description column on your far left and many number columns to the right of it.

Firms often use journals, and office supply stores sell them. Just show the clerk the last few paragraphs, and he or she will know exactly what you want. Journals are expensive, so finish reading this chapter before you buy one. Many denominations provide a book that serves as a journal.

After you have bought your adding machine and a journal, you can begin. The first step is most difficult because it depends on the existing records. You must find out exactly how much money the church has, including the balance of each fund. You will need to know the checking account's reconciled balance, which is last month's ending

Fig. 4.2. Sample journal page showing recorded receipts

PLEASANT VALLEY COMMUNITY CHURCH
June 1996

	1 CASH	2 Church Operating	3 Building	4 Evangelism	5 Employee	6 Page Fund	7 Piano/Organ Fund	8 Vacation Bible Sch.	9 Youth Activity
Balances from May	19385.97	1021.376	301.691	677.950	3112.160	781.60	919.19	112.681	531.60
Receipts:									
Campbells	80000		5000	20000		10000		5000	2000
Condons	15000	15000					5000		
Cowan, Ann	7575	7575							
Cowan, Bryan	40000		10000	30000					
Donaldsons	3500					3500			
Langleys	35000			15000		10000	10000		
McKnights	42500	20000	22500						
Mallards	10000	10000							
Procters	60000		30000	30000					
Shoafs	10000	20000							
Smith	25000						25000		
Taylors	50000	10000	10000			5000	10000	5000	10000
Westfalls	40000	10000	10000	10000		10000			
Zuber, Emma	985			985					
Loose offering	11321	11321							
Total Deposits	548701	211916	87500	105985	-0-	38500	65000	700.00	30000
Balance before checks	2497498	1233212	389191	1734.35	3112.160	116660	156919	226681	831160

reconciled balance. (See appendix 2 for information on balancing bank accounts.)

After you know your checking account balance, finding each fund's balance is simple. Using all you know about the church, find the amount in each fund except the general fund. After finding the funds' balances, subtract them from the total cash. This will give you the general fund balance. When you finish, the total of the funds equals the amount of cash.

Once you find your starting balances, open your journal to the first two-page spread. The description column is on the far left, and columns cover the rest of that page and the facing page. Write at the very top your church's name and the month and year you are working with. Do not write the current date. Follow figures 4.2 and 4.3.

Next, write a heading at the top of each column. Label the first column "Cash." This is where you record what happens in your checking account. This column adds deposits and subtracts checks.

Label the second column "General Fund" and the other columns with the names of the other funds. Each fund's column tracks what happens with that fund.

Next, write the cash balance on the first line of the cash column and each fund's balance on its respective first line (fig. 4.2). The fund columns' total should always equal the cash column. Check often to make sure this is so.

RECEIPTS

Let us look for a moment at receipts (figure 4.3 shows a sample receipt). Have your church print shop provide two copies of each receipt. One copy is yours, and the other is the donor's.

Every week record the gifts on the receipt. Record the total amount and the funds given to. After the month ends, add the total monthly gifts and add the specific funds given to. The receipt's fund totals should equal the member's total gifts.

Fig. 4.3. Sample receipt

Pleasant Valley Community Church
"Making Christ Known"

CAMPBELLS

FUND	1st	2nd	3rd	4th	5th	Total
General	50~		50~	50~		150~
Building	50~					50~
Evangelism	100~		100~			200~
Youth Activities	100~			100~		200~
Flower Fund						
Lay Ministries						
Hudson Taylor						
New Organ				50~		50~
Vac. Bible School			50~			50~
Total	300~		200~	200~		700~

Receipt for ___ JUNE ___

___ IRA PLATT ___
Treasurer

LOOSE OFFERINGS

Also prepare a separate loose offerings receipt. Often the loose offerings belong to the general fund, but the board may choose other funds to receive the money. For example, they may decide that on certain days the youth get it. Or other days the building fund may get it. Whatever fund receives it does not matter; simply prepare a receipt as you would for any member. Label this receipt "loose offerings."

The total of all the receipts should equal the week's bank deposit.

RECORDING RECEIPTS

At month's end record each receipt into the journal. Write the donor's name in the description column, the total amount the donor gave for the month in the cash column, and the totals for each fund in the respective fund columns. The journal in figure 4.2 records the Campbells' receipt.

Treat the loose offerings receipt like all the rest. The journal in figure 4.2 shows this as the last receipt.

Add the columns. When you are adding do not add the balances carried over from the preceding month. All you want is the total deposits for the present month. Add each of the fund column totals. Make sure that this total equals the cash column total. If these are not equal, find your mistake. There are three ways you could have erred: (1) You made out an individual receipt incorrectly, (2) you copied a receipt incorrectly, or (3) you added incorrectly.

After you balance the receipts, add the deposits to the opening balances written on the first line. Again, make sure the column totals for the funds equal the cash column. Figure 4.2 shows how your journal should look at this point.

Fig. 4.4. Sample journal page

Pleasant Valley Community Church
June 1986

Date		Payee / Description	Cash	1 Church Operating	2 Building	3 Evangelism	4 Employees	5 Poor Fund	6 New Organ Fund	7 Vacation Bible School	8 Youth Activities	9
		Balance Forward	24879478	12133292	3691191	1173935	3121160	1116660	1567179	214681	931160
		Checks:									
6/3		Pleasant Valley Auto 316	3896	3896							
6/3		P. Valley Electric Co-op 317	19860	19860							
6/5		John Poser (nac) 318	10000					10000			
6/5		Ace Electric (rewiring) 319	67340		67340						
6/14		Johnsons Paper Supplies 310	11911	11911							
6/15		Bible Bookstore 321	30000	15000		5000					10000
6/30		Otto Stiger (Reimb.) 322	25096	25096						25096	
6/30		Pastor Kincaid 323	148631				148631				
6/30		Pastor Luree 324	123299				123299				
6/30		Bella's Flowers 325	17631	17631							
		Total Checks	4599794	70378	67340	5000	271930	10000	-0-	250996	10000
			20277754	1162914	3218151	1684935	40230	106660	1569179	(2415)	73116
		Insurance Draft	(19860)	(19860)							
		Service Charge	(915)	(985)							
		Interest	7860	9860							
		McKnight's NSF check	(10000)						(10000)		
		Reconciled Balances	20006769	1151929	3218151	1684935	40230	106660	1469179	(2415)	73116
		Board Transfers		(344345)		30000	279930		30000	2415	10000
		June's Ending Balances	20006769	9875589	3218151	1984935	3121160	1066660	1769179	-0-	931160

RECORDING CHECKS

Now record the month's checks as shown in figure 4.4. Simply drop down a few lines and record the checks written, working from the checkbook. Enter the date of the check in the far left column, the check number and payee in the description column, and the amount in the cash column. Also enter the amount under the specific fund the check was written from.

If a check is written for more than one fund, divide the total among the funds. Suppose that a check for $300 is written to the Bible Bookstore. Of this amount, $100 is for youth work, $50 is for soulwinning, and the rest is for general church needs. Check number 321 in figure 4.4 illustrates this. You would record the check this way: Write "Bible Bookstore" and the check number in the description column. Under the cash column write $300, under youth work write $100, under soulwinning write $50, and under church general fund write $150. Keep the funds' amount equal to the cash amount.

Now add the amounts of the checks in all columns. This total should equal the check total for all funds.

After you balance, *subtract* the totals for the checks from the last column totals made after the deposits. Again, make sure all the fund columns' totals equal the cash column total.

Now balance the bank statement to your cash column. When balanced, the cash column will equal the checking account balance. See appendix 2 for instructions on balancing the bank statement with the journal.

TRANSFERS

After you have reconciled the cash column to the bank statement, record any interfund transfers. These transfers must be approved by the board. Nothing you do will change the cash column; only the fund totals will change. Suppose the board approves a hundred–dollar transfer from the general fund to the youth work fund. You would record this transfer by writing "$100.00" under the general fund column and putting brackets around it, and "$100.00" under the youth work fund without brackets. Bracketing signifies that the amount has been subtracted.

Your monthly record keeping is complete: (1) the cash column balances with the bank statement, (2) the funds' totals show what the funds have at month's end, and (3) all the fund columns equal the cash column.

5 | A NEVER-ENDING MAZE: TAXES

Two A.M. All is quiet in Pastor Jim's house. Everyone sleeps. Suddenly a blood curdling scream cuts through the air. Pastor Jim is having a nightmare—his third this week. Tonight he twists in a never-ending maze, turning this way and that, ever circling back on his track. Last night he tried to untangle a ton of kite string, and the night before he wandered lost in the California freeway system.

Pastor Jim's nightmares started last week when he studied the tax laws on contributions. Ever since then he has mumbled about being lost and confused. You can hardly blame him. The tax laws grow every year and confuse the mind. Congress passes laws, the Internal Revenue Service enforces the laws, and the courts interpret and settle conflicts. All this churns out a tax law maze.

Every April articles appear about how difficult it is to get a straight answer. Taxpayers make repeated calls to the IRS and get different answers to the same question! Even CPAs and tax attorneys give conflicting advice. If it confuses the financial experts, what is a church leader to do?

Why should a church leader know tax law? First, the church is probably tax exempt, and you must guard that tax-exempt status. Many people think that the church is tax exempt because of some legal right. This is false. The government grants tax-exempt status to a church. Misuse it, and they take it away.

Second, some gifts reduce taxes and some do not. You

need to understand tax laws so you can wisely help your members make their giving decisions.

Third, simple tax law knowledge protects the church from crooked people who try to use the church's tax-exempt status to cheat on their taxes. Being careful saves the church from shame later.

Finally, church members make many gifts. You need to know tax laws so that you can use them to reduce your taxes. The Bible says not to cheat on taxes. On the other hand, honestly reducing your taxes frees money to be spent elsewhere in God's work.

TAX-EXEMPT STATUS

Churches come under tax law section 501(c)3. This code says churches do not have to pay taxes on the gifts they receive and the gifts are deductible for the givers. The law does not make a church apply for tax-exempt status.

It is best, however, for the church to get a ruling from the IRS saying that it is tax exempt. This prevents possible questions and embarrassment later. Applying for tax-exempt status needs to be done by someone who knows how to do it. Perhaps you have a CPA or tax lawyer in your parish who can help. The following paragraphs show the way to apply for tax-exempt status.

Your church may have already gone through the process for receiving tax-exempt status. Often a parent organization does this one time for all its churches. Your diocese, conference, association, etc., may do this chore. But you may need to read this section if you want to start a ministry such as a school or an outreach association. Such ministries may not automatically fall under your church's tax-exempt status.

This is the process: File a form with the IRS that describes your church. Attach the church's articles of incorporation and bylaws. If you do not have articles of incorporation or bylaws, hire an attorney. A lawyer will prepare them for approval by your secretary of state. This will make your church a separate legal entity. The bylaws show how the decisions in the church are made, what to do in disputes, and what to do with the church's assets if it fails. This is sometimes called the church's constitution.

After you mail the form describing your church to the IRS, expect the IRS to want more information or for you to change your bylaws. Usually it is a small change in what will happen to the assets if the church fails; the IRS wants them to go to some other tax-exempt group. When satisfied, the IRS will mail a tentative approval good for several years. After several years you will have to go through the process again. Then the IRS will give you final approval.

One reason you should apply for tax-exempt status is because the IRS is after phony churches that abuse the system to avoid taxes. In our day it is quite common for a person to set up a "church" and declare himself as high priest. He is the only member, and he donates all his property to the "church" and takes a deduction. Each year he donates all his salary so that he has no income tax. The IRS has declared war on this scam. You could get caught in the cross fire, so apply for tax-exempt status. Then your ministry will not be mistaken for one of those so-called "churches."

DEDUCTIBLE OR NONDEDUCTIBLE?

The very first tax law allowed for the deduction of gifts to churches on the donor's tax return. Today people abuse this in the oddest ways. Some deduct payments to their children. Some overstate the value of donated Bibles. Some deduct the price of tickets to boxing matches. Some even deduct an amount they intended to give to a church. The list goes on and on.

Personal deductions must meet three criteria: (1) They must be to a qualified organization, (2) there must be no direct benefit to the donor, and (3) there must be no strings attached.

A Qualified Organization

A tax-exempt religious organization in the United States is a qualified organization. A gift to a church in Brazil is not deductible. However, a gift to the general fund of a U.S. church that, among other things, supports churches in Brazil is deductible. A gift to a poor person is not deductible, but a gift to a church that tends to poor people is. A gift directly to a needy church member is not deductible, but a payment to a minister's fund to help poor members is. A gift made to the poor through a committee is not deductible, but a gift to a tax-exempt corporation that cares for the poor is deductible.

No Direct Benefit to the Donor

If a donor benefits from a gift, it is not deductible. For example, a gift to a church to reduce your child's church school tuition is not deductible. Only general donations are deductible. A gift to send your son's choir to Europe is not deductible, but a contribution to cover sheet music cost is. A payment to a missionary society for the expenses of your missionary son is not deductible, but general donations are. If you give a building to a church but the church buys the land from you, you receive no deduction. A donation made to attend a marriage seminar is not deductible. A portion of a "donation at the door" for a spaghetti supper or concert is deductible. In such cases you must deduct the amount given minus the fair value of the thing received. For instance, radio ministers often send a book to everyone who gives twenty dollars or more. The deductible amount is only the amount sent in that is above the book's price in the bookstore. Suppose a book sells in bookstores for eight dollars. A twenty-dollar check results in a twelve-dollar deduction.

A raffle ticket purchase is not deductible even if it says, "$5 donation."

No Strings Attached

For a gift to be deductible, it must be unconditional. The giver must yield ownership and control of the gift to the church. For example, Sister Sally wants to give her piano to the church. But since it has "been in the family," she may want to get it back. This is not a deduction for Sally. It is just a loan.

Or perhaps Brother Tom buys camping equipment for the church's Boy Scout troop. Only the Boy Scouts use the gear, but he never gives it over to their control. It is not a donation because he can take it back whenever he wants to.

Members often specify how to use a gift. Betty Jo donates land but says she wants it back if the church does not use it to build on. It is deductible only after the church builds on the site.

Sometimes the terms simply ensure that the church handles the gift properly, but other times the terms are a way to control the church. Brother Ebenezer donates a sound system and says, "I'll take it out if you use it with guitar music." If the church is not likely to use it with guitar music, he can deduct the donation.

Allowing the church to use property is not deductible. Sister Smith loaned the church a house for a parsonage. She cannot deduct the rent she could have earned. At first this seems unfair. It is fair, however, because if she rents the house, she earns taxable income. If she donates the rent income to the church, she has a deduction. The income and the deduction offset each other. This is the same as if she had allowed the church to use the house in the first place.

In the same way, a person cannot deduct the value of time given to the church. This is true even if it is easy to put a dollar value on the time. For instance, Brother John, the lawyer, cannot deduct the time he spends doing legal work for the church. He does not count any income for the time he spends.

In order for a donation to be deductible, it must be wholly turned over to the church with no strings attached. Tax law would be simple if it neatly fit into such one-sentence absolutes, but there are always exceptions to any rule.

You can deduct the cost of buying and cleaning uniforms, vestments, or choir robes even if you keep them. The uniforms must be unfit for ordinary use. So deduct the cost of a Salvation Army uniform or a Boy Scout uniform, since they are not suitable for ordinary use. If a church music group buys matching blue skirts, they are not deductible because the skirts are suitable for other uses.

Similar rules deal with books bought for use at church. If the books are useful only in the service, deduct their cost. An example is prayer books used by lay readers who lead out in the service. A book bought to study at Wednesday night Bible study is not deductible. General donations to the church library are deductible.

Deducting travel is confusing. You can deduct the cost of trips taken as a service to the church. This includes airline tickets and hotel cost. Deduct only 80 percent of the cost of meals. An important catch is that you can deduct the trip only if there is not a major element of personal pleasure. Get ready for some hair-splitting. If you take a youth group to the beach, you can deduct it if you are on duty a major part of the time. But if you have only nominal duties, say you drive a group to the beach house and then go on to your own vacation, forget it. If you go to a church convention and spend the entire day at church meetings but spend the evening at the theater, the trip is still deductible.

Suppose you go on a church building project to South America. Half of the day you pound nails into a new church, and the other half you sightsee. You will receive no deduction, even if you work very hard every morning. But weekend sightseeing is okay.

On trips or around town you can deduct for mileage for your car. Find out the current rate per mile. You can deduct the actual gas and oil cost if it is more than the current rate. You cannot deduct travel back and forth from church unless, for example, you are taking the elderly to church. It must be mileage driven in some service for the church, not for some service you are receiving.

WHEN IS A GIFT DEDUCTIBLE?

Usually you may deduct a gift when it is given, but there are a few particulars. First, as shown above, you may deduct a gift only after the church fulfills any restrictions on the gift. Restrictions unlikely to come into play do not prohibit the deduction immediately.

Second, you must give the gift before you deduct it. A pledge is not deductible; nor is a postdated check. A promissory note to the church is not deductible until it is paid. A gift of real estate is not deductible until after the closing.

HOW MUCH OF A GIFT IS DEDUCTIBLE?

You may deduct gifts equal to half of your income. Brother Steve has an adjusted gross income of $50,000 and contributions of $40,000. He will deduct $25,000 this year and carry forward the $15,000 that he did not deduct. He may deduct the leftover $15,000 next year. The 50 percent limit will still apply in the second year. He has five years to use up all his contribution, or it will be lost.

You may think this problem does not happen very often, but it does. It has been said that J. C. Penney donated 50 percent of his income. Often an elderly person who has a low income donates a large portion to the church. A person selling land at a loss may give a portion of the money from the sale. Inherited money is not taxable income, so a person donating a portion of an inheritance could easily hit the limit.

HOW MUCH DOES A GIFT COST ME?

You hear it all the time: "He only did it for the tax break!" Sure, people donate for reasons other than the right reason. They give to impress other church members or friends. They give to make up for sins they hope God will forgive. They give in an effort to earn points with God. But nobody (with any sense) gives to save taxes. You cannot save money by giving.

Consider Sister Cathy. Suppose she is in a make-believe 90 percent tax bracket. She gives $100,000 to the church. The $100,000 gift saves her $90,000 in taxes, so the gift cost her $10,000 after taxes. The gift is not as big of a sacrifice as it at first appears. However, she does have $10,000 less. There is no way to make money by giving it to the church.

Sister Cathy's case shows the way the government helps churches. The church gets $100,000. At this make-believe tax rate, it only cost Sister Cathy $10,000. Where did the other $90,000 come from? From the government. In a real sense the government operates on a matching basis. It says, "We will match a certain portion of the contributions given by our citizens. We match a higher portion for the wealthy." Some people use this to attack the government for helping religion. The other side argues that churches help society, so it is worth the tax cost.

When Congress cut tax rates, many church leaders worried that people would give less, since the after-tax cost of gifts would be higher. By lowering taxes the government lowered its share of the gift. As a whole, however, changes in the tax law do not reduce the giving level.

A NOTE TO MINISTERS

Ministers are a tax "no man's land"—part employee, part self-employed. They often make gifts to the church. Tithing may be a job requirement. Perhaps they buy supplies or equipment out of their own pockets to help programs get off the ground. Are these gifts business expenses or contributions? What difference does it make?

Are you a self-employed minister for tax purposes? Most ministers are. Then it is better to call payments to the church business expenses. Subtract the payments on your Schedule C form to reduce your self-employment tax. But do so only if those payments are truly business expenses. Business expenses are "ordinary and necessary to carry out your job. Buying your own office supplies or vestments are ordinary and necessary. Giving to the building fund is probably not ordinary and necessary.

Some churches require ministers to tithe. Would this be an ordinary and necessary part of doing business as a minister in your church? There is no clear answer; it is something for the courts to decide.

If you are not self-employed, call everything possible a contribution. Only the employee expenses that exceed 2 percent of your income are deductible.

DEFERRED GIVING

Never heard of deferred giving? Most likely you have, but not under its real name. An example shows it best: Brother Hank works hard to build up a hardware business. Then he sells his business so he can do self-supporting missionary work during his last years. He faces a huge tax on his gain from the sale of his business, so he needs a deduction. But he also needs money to live on. Hank plans to give his money to the church when he dies, but right now he needs to invest the money and live off the interest. This is one case where the tax law lets Hank have his cake and eat it, too.

Brother Hank solves his problem by setting up a trust. His money is put in the care of some other person or organization, such as a bank. Hank is the trustor. The other person or organization is the trustee. The trustor says what to do with the money, and the trustee does it. In Hank's trust he gets the interest that his money earns, and his church gets what is left when he dies.

Hank gets a deduction right away. He deducts the present value of the final gift to the church. Present value is easy to understand. Suppose Hank is fifty-five years old and puts $100,000 in his trust. He can deduct about $78,000. This amount comes off an IRS chart. It is what he would invest now to have $100,000 when he dies. Hanks $100,000 given when he dies is worth $78,000 today, so he deducts $78,000 now.

All this present-value talk may distract you from the main point. Hank can keep using his money, so to speak, and get a deduction now when he needs it, not when he dies. How wonderful! It is wonderful for Hank because he pays less tax in the year he sells the store. If he pays fewer taxes, there is more in the trust earning interest for him to live on. It is wonderful for the church because Hank pays less tax, and the church gets more when he dies.

This is not a sneaking, cheating tax dodge. Congress allows it to inspire giving. The IRS strictly controls how the trust is set up. For instance, it must be "irrevocable." Hank cannot back out for any reason, so even if the church turns wicked, it gets what is in the trust when Hank dies.

There are four different deferred giving plans: (1) remainder annuity trust, (2) remainder unitrust, (3) pooled income fund, and (4) life insurance gifts.

The remainder annuity trust pays a fixed amount each year to a specific person. Hank's trust is set up to pay him five hundred dollars per month. When he dies it will pay his wife five hundred dollars per month until she dies. The remainder will go to the church.

A unitrust is like an annuity trust, but instead of paying a fixed amount, it pays a percentage of the balance in the trust to the trustor. The unitrust is similar to earning interest. If the trust goes up in value, the amount paid to Hank goes up. It also pays Hank's wife after he dies. Then the remainder goes to the church.

A pooled income fund mingles the donation with similar donations from others. The pool earns interest and divides the earnings among the people who donated the money. When people die, their share goes to the church.

Many people have life insurance policies they no longer need. For instance, Brother Fred bought an insurance policy when he was a young father and needed to provide for his two children. Now that his children are grown, he can give the policy to the church. He can deduct the policy's replacement value when he gives it. When he dies the church will receive his death benefits. Any premiums he pays after he gives the policy to the church are also deductible.

AN IMPORTANT WARNING

When some ministers talk about tax laws, they speak with an authority that befits their position: "Such and such is deductible." "I read this book on church finances, and it said. . . ."

Now listen to accountants and attorneys talk. They say: "I think it is deductible." "Usually it is handled this way." They use plenty of modifiers and use such phrases as "I think," "usually," "most of the time," and "it's my understanding." Accountants and lawyers talk this way because they know there is a real chance that they are wrong. Tax laws change with new laws, with every new IRS rule, and with every tax court decision. You cannot be too sure in taxes.

This chapter covers only the tax laws that have existed solidly through the years. Focus on the laws' themes instead of being specific. For example, you saw that gift with strings attached are not deductible. Such a theme is unlikely to change. If you focus on whether such and such is deductible, you miss the chapter's point. Tax laws change, and probably every example in this chapter has an exception buried in some court case or regulation, so use this chapter as general guidance only.

The next chapter is also about taxes. It deals with receiving property gifts.

If you are reading this chapter before you go to bed, recite the Twenty-third Psalm. It might help you with the nightmares.

6 | ASK AND IT SHALL BE GIVEN: PROPERTY GIFTS

Poor Pastor Jim. What a mess he is in! A few months ago he noticed that Shulerville was the perfect city for a new church. The new interstate highway was changing Shulerville from a small farming town into a blossoming suburb, so he rented a meeting hall, held meetings, and started a new church. The church met each week in the gym of Shulerville High's Fighting Demons.

Right away a building committee met. The new church needed a building. (You should try worshiping in the Fighting Demons' gym!) They started looking for land, and that is when the problems began. Even the smallest piece of land cost over $100,000—too much for Pastor Jim's tiny church! The real estate boom had reached Shulerville before Jim had. Poor Pastor Jim. What a mess!

Pastor Jim prays and decides there is only one solution: he is going to ask someone to give land to the church. After all, he is asking for God, not for himself.

Jim finds an ideal lot. A few years ago it was a pasture. Now the pasture is a subdivision, and the lot for the church sits right at the entrance. The farmer who owns it could easily sell it for $150,000, but the land is not for sale. That does not bother Jim—he does not want to buy the land; he wants the farmer to give it.

There is another side to this coin. The farmer is also in a mess. The whole pasture cost him $1,000 back in '39. He received almost a million dollars when he sold it for the subdivision. Now he must pay taxes on this profit. He owes the IRS a lot of money. What is even worse, the new tax law taxes the capital gain as ordinary income.

The farmer has two options: he can sell the land to help pay his taxes, or he can give the land to the church and get a tax deduction. He is in a 30 percent tax bracket. The land that Jim wants cost the farmer $1,000. If the farmer sells the land, his tax bill will go up another $44,700:

Income from the sale	$150,000
Cost to the farmer	1,000
Capital Gain	$149,000
Extra Taxes 30%	$44,700

Selling it will leave him $105,300 after taxes. That is $150,000 from the sale minus the $44,700 extra taxes. If the farmer gives the church the land, he will reduce his tax bill by $45,000, or 30 percent of the land's fair market value.

So again, the farmer has two options: sell the land and have $105,300 to use to pay his taxes, or give the land to the church and have $45,000 less in taxes.

At first Jim thought he was asking for land worth $150,000, because this is what the church would pay if it bought it. But Jim is not asking for $150,000. It costs the farmer $60,300 to give the land. This is the land's after-tax value ($105,300) minus the tax savings from the gift ($45,000).

The $60,300 is a real cost to the farmer. He has $60,300 less to spend on himself. So Jim's appeal is based on the farmer's goodwill, not on the tax benefits. There is no way to make a profit by giving. However, Jim feels better knowing that he is asking the farmer to give to the tune of $60,300 instead of $150,000.

ANOTHER CASE

To change the case, suppose the farmer turns Pastor Jim down. With relentless tenacity he finds Bill who will give some land. The land is worth $150,000. It cost Bill $1,000. (These are the same as the farmer's figures.) There is one drawback. It is twenty acres in an industrial park, not a place for a church. Bill has two options: he can sell the land and donate the money to the church, or he can donate the land to the church and the church can sell the land. Either way the church has $150,000. However, the choice he makes affects the gift's after-tax cost. Look at this table:

	Gift of land	Sale of land and gift of proceeds
Pretax value of gift	$150,000	$150,000
Tax savings from the gift ($150,000 x 30%)	−45,000	−45,000
Tax paid on capital gain (from the farmer's figures above)		+44,700
After-tax "cost" of gift	$105,000	$149,700

If Bill sells the land, he must pay the tax on the capital gain ($44,700). Yet he will have $45,000 fewer taxes because of the gift. So selling the land and giving the money to the church cost him $149,700.

Giving the land to the church will cost Bill $105,000. He has the same tax benefits from the gift, but he avoids the tax on the capital gain. Thus it is better for Bill to give the land to the church. It cost him $105,000, and the church has land worth $150,000.

Here are four warnings. First, Bill must not find a buyer before giving the land to the church. Often the owner finds a buyer for the land then delivers the land and the buyer to the church. The church gets the land and sells it to the buyer. This is not proper in the IRS's eyes, so warn donors to avoid finding a buyer before giving land.

Second, these examples apply only to capital gain property such as land, buildings, and stocks. They do not apply to ordinary income property such as merchandise or equipment. The next section deals with gifts of ordinary income property. Usually donors of this property can deduct only the cost paid for the property.

Third, the examples use a 30 percent tax bracket. At the time of this writing, the highest rate for federal taxes is 32 percent. State tax rates make it even higher. In any case, lower tax brackets give smaller tax savings, and higher tax brackets give greater savings.

Finally, never do the tax expert's job. There are many traps in the tax laws. This chapter's purpose is to give you guidelines. When you ask for land, offer to pay the donor's CPA or tax lawyer to figure the after-tax cost.

THINGS GIVEN TO THE CHURCH

People give all sorts of things to the church: old clothes, books, cars and pianos—the list goes on and on. Also the church gets such things as groceries and hardware from stores. Some things the church uses, some it sells, and some it throws away. Dozens of tax scams float around in this arena. Imagine how hard it is for Congress to make laws to control such donations.

Someone may ask "How much can I deduct for giving ordinary things like old clothes or pianos?" The answer is easy. Deduct what you can sell it for. Finding the value of used cars, pianos, and clothes is easy. Ignore sentimental value and the cost when it was new. Your favorite shirt cost thirty dollars. You wore it when your baby came home from the hospital. Now a new one costs forty dollars, but the best you could get for your shirt at a garage sale is two or three dollars. Therefore that is all you deduct if you give it.

Gifts out of inventory are about the same. Brother Greg, the grocer, gives the church food. He deducts only what it costs him. He sells beans for three dollars, but he deducts only the two dollars they cost him. Thus he is kept from making a profit by giving.

There is an exception. It is a little cloudy, but it is worth knowing if your ministry involves care for "the ill, the needy, or infants."

Brother Greg sells beans for $3.00. Since he pays $2.00

for them, his normal profit is $1.00. If he gives the beans away for, say, a church picnic, he can deduct only the $2.00 he paid for them. But if he gives the beans to a project that cares for the ill, the needy, or infants, he can deduct $2.50. This is his cost plus half of his normal profit.

The donor must be a regular corporation (not an S Corp.). Many businesses are corporations, so even your corner grocery may be able to benefit from these rules.

Suppose your church wants to open a soup kitchen. You have workers and a kitchen, but you have no food. You must find a food store to give you the food. You think you could start with $10,000 in food. A food store chain is considering giving the food. Here are its figures:

Value of the food needed	$10,000
Store's cost	−7,500
Normal profit	$2,500
Store's cost	$7,500
Plus half the profit	1,250
Total deduction	$8,750
Times the tax rate	50%
Tax savings from gift	$4,375
Out-of-pocket cost	$7,500
Less tax savings	4,375
After-tax cost of gift	$3,125

A $10,000 gift in food cost the store only $3,125. This is based on a company in the maximum tax bracket and using a 25 percent markup. A lower tax bracket or markup raises the after-tax cost to the company.

WHAT ARE THE CHURCH'S DUTIES?

Receiving property gifts is risky. Many people give churches property and overstate its value when they deduct it on their tax return. To control such abuse Congress has passed far-reaching rules. The church and its donors must follow these rules.

Receipts

Churches must give complete receipts for property they receive. A good receipt gives the church's name and address, the date the property was received, and where the property is. It also shows the gift's terms. For instance, a member may limit the gift for "use only in the church." The receipt must state the value of any premiums (e.g., books, tapes) the church gives to the donor.

A good receipt also describes the property the church receives. This last rule is most difficult. Receipts for higher valued gifts require more details. Receipts for donated clothes may simply state, "Six shirts." A receipt for a car may say, "1988 Volvo GL with electric windows, air conditioning, and leather seats, in fair condition." Saying "1988 Volvo" is not enough. A receipt for land should include a copy of the legal description from the deed.

A receipt need not show a value for the property. However, it must be described so that someone can set a fair value. A church should avoid saying anything that overstates the property value.

Forms 8282 and 8283

There are special rules to follow if the value of a property gift is over $500 or over $5000. (These limits change over time, so check on the current amount.) Two special IRS forms come into play, Form 8282 and Form 8283. Copies are shown on pages 66 and 67.

Suppose Brother North donates equipment worth more than $500. He fills out Form 8283 and sends it in with his regular tax return. This will help the IRS evaluate the fairness of the amount he deducts.

Form **8282**
(Rev. August 1988)
Department of the Treasury
Internal Revenue Service

Donee Information Return

(Sale, Exchange, or Other Disposition of Donated Property)
▶ See instructions on back.

OMB No. 1545-0908
Expires 3-31-90

Give Copy to Donor

Please Print or Type

Charitable organization (donee) name	Employer identification number
Number and street	
City or town, state, and ZIP code	

Note: *If you are the original donee, DO NOT complete Part II, or column (c) of Part III*

Part I Information on ORIGINAL DONOR, and DONEE YOU GAVE THE PROPERTY TO

1(a) Name of the original donor of (first person to give) the property	(b) Identification number

Complete 2(a)–2(d) only if you gave this property to another charitable organization (successor donee):

2(a) Name of charitable organization	(b) Identification number (EIN)
(c) Address (number and street)	
(d) City or town, state, and ZIP code	

Part II Information on PREVIOUS DONEES—Complete this part only if you were not the first donee to receive the property.
If you were the second donee, leave item 4 blank. If you were a third or later donee, then complete both items 3 and 4.
In item 4 give information on the preceding donee (the one who gave you the gift).

3(a) Name of original donee	(b) Identification number (EIN)
(c) Address (number and street)	
(d) City or town, state, and ZIP code	

4(a) Name of preceding donee	(b) Identification number (EIN)
(c) Address (number and street)	
(d) City or town, state, and ZIP code	

Part III Information on DONATED PROPERTY

(a) Description of donated property sold, exchanged, or otherwise disposed of (attach a separate sheet if more space is needed)	(b) Date you received the item(s)	(c) Date the first donee received the item(s) (if you weren't the first)	(d) Date item(s) sold, exchanged, or otherwise disposed of	(e) Amount received upon disposition

For Paperwork Reduction Act Notice, see instructions on back.

Form **8282** (Rev. 8-88)

| Form **8283** (Rev. October 1987) Department of the Treasury Internal Revenue Service | **Noncash Charitable Contributions** ► Attach to your Federal income tax return if the total claimed value of all property contributed exceeds $500. ► See separate Instructions. | OMB No. 1545-0908 Expires 9-30-88 Attachment Sequence No. **55** |

Name(s) as shown on your income tax return | Identification number

Section A Include in Section A **only** items (or groups of similar items) which have a claimed value of $5,000 or less per item or group and certain publicly traded securities (see Instructions).

Part I Information on Donated Property

1

	(a) Name and address of the donee organization	(b) Description of donated property (attach a separate sheet if more space is needed)
A		
B		
C		
D		
E		

Note: Columns (d), (e), and (f) do not have to be completed for items with a value of $500 or less.

	(c) Date of the contribution	(d) Date acquired by donor (mo., yr.)	(e) How acquired by donor	(f) Donor's cost or adjusted basis	(g) Fair market value	(h) Method used to determine the fair market value
A						
B						
C						
D						
E						

Part II Other Information—Complete question 2 if you gave less than an entire interest in property listed in Part I. Complete question 3 if restrictions were attached to a contribution listed in Part I.

2 If less than the entire interest in the property is contributed during the year, complete the following:

(a) Enter letter from Part I which identifies the property _____ . (Attach a separate statement if Part II applies to more than one property.)

(b) Total amount claimed as a deduction for the property listed in Part I for this tax year _____ ; for any prior tax year(s) _____ .

(c) Name and address of each organization to which any such contribution was made in a prior year (complete only if different from the donee organization above).

Charitable organization (donee) name

Number and street

City or town, state, and ZIP code

(d) The place where any tangible property is located or kept. _____

(e) Name of any person, other than the donee organization, having actual possession of the property. _____

3 If conditions were attached to any contribution listed in Part I, answer the following questions:

	Yes	No
(a) Is there a restriction either temporarily or permanently on the donee's right to use or dispose of the donated property?		
(b) Did you give to anyone (other than the donee organization or another organization participating with the donee organization in cooperative fundraising) the right to the income from the donated property or to the possession of the property, including the right to vote donated securities, to acquire the property by purchase or otherwise, or to designate the person having such income, possession, or right to acquire?		
(c) Is there a restriction limiting the donated property for a particular use?		

For Paperwork Reduction Act Notice, see separate Instructions. Form **8283** (Rev. 10-87)

If the gift is worth more than $5000, someone named by the church board must fill in Form 8283's section B, part 1. Usually this is the treasurer or the minister. It shows the gift's receipt.

Form 8282 applies only to gifts worth more than $5000. The church must fill in Form 8282 if it sells or gives away the property within two years from when it is received. The church must send a copy of Form 8282 to the IRS and to the donor. This form names the donor and shows how much the church sold the donated property for. This helps the IRS decide if the value the donor put on Form 8283 is fair.

Who signs Forms 8282 and 8283 for the church? Usually the church board names the church treasurer or the pastor. Someone needs to keep track of donated property for several years, so appoint a stable person. If the church often changes pastors, appoint the treasurer. If the church often changes treasurers, appoint the pastor. Whoever does it must be careful. He or she should keep a folder with copies of all signed 8283 forms. Every three months or so the folder should be reviewed to find anything the church sold, gave away, or threw away within two years of its receipt. A Form 8282 must be prepared for these items and sent to the IRS within 125 days after something has been sold. Remove old 8283 forms from your folder when they are two years old to keep the folder current.

How often does the church receive something that is worth more than $5000? When it does, how often does the church sell it? It happens more often than you think. Often God convicts people to give up something they value to build meekness and self-sacrifice. What people give can range from cars to coin collections, from designer dresses to jewelry. Usually a church intends to sell the donated property from the minute it receives it.

This also applies in some less obvious ways. For example, if Brother Jones buys an organ and gives it to the church, he prepares a Form 8283. If the church sells the organ within two years, it sends in Form 8282. If Brother Bill gives land for a new church, he prepares Form 8283. If the church sells the land a year later because it can not get it properly zoned, it sends in Form 8282.

These rules about property gifts are tough but worth knowing. The pastor that looks only for the money in the offering plate to support the church is missing great things. After all, the Bible says, "Ask and it will be given." (Matt. 7:7).

7 | *COUNTING THE COST: BUDGETS 101*

Eleven P.M. The board meeting started at seven. What a night! Every time Pastor Jim says, "White," Brother Ebenezer says, "Black." Pastor Jim feels like busting Brother Ebenezer's nose. His only hope is Christ. He remembers what Christ suffered on his behalf: how Christ endured lies—shot at him like missiles of hate. Pastor Jim wonders if Jesus ever had a board meeting. The meeting is about to end, just one more agenda item. "I have one little thing to do and then we can go home," Pastor Jim says. "We need a budget committee to make a budget for us."

Brother Ebenezer says: "What do we need a budget for? We've never had one before. We've gotten along just fine. It's just another waste of time. Look how much time you already have taken with this meeting!"

Pastor Jim counts to ten. One. Remember the lies against Jesus. Two. Remember how Shimei threw rocks at David. Three. "He was wounded for our transgressions." Four. "By his stripes we are healed." The ringing in Jim's ears stops. His blood eases its pressure on his brain. His arms relax. He appears to the others to be in quiet thought.

Then Jim says: "You're right. I shouldn't do something new without saying why. Let's meet next week, and I'll explain why we need a budget. If you want, we'll use that time to get started making a budget. Then you can see first-hand what goes into one."

Jim's work is cut out for him. The other churches he

pastored had a budget program in place. Those churches expected it. But why? Why do churches bother with budgets? Are budgets just a modern tradition, or do they serve a real purpose? Do all churches need them? Are there nonfinancial reasons to have a budget? What is the best way to make a budget? Do budgets show lagging faith? Where does faith come in?

First, a budget is more than a financial tool. Is controlling expenses the only reason you make a budget? If so, it is not worth the trouble. What makes budgeting valuable is that it forces a church to evaluate programs and set priorities. In one sense, the dollars given to a program show the program's value to the church.

Churches without budgets operate like this: Sister Sally wants new hymnals, so she brings her request to the board. The board sees the need and checks to see if the church has enough money. If it does, they spend it on her project. If not, nothing is done.

No effort is made to rank the church's needs. The first request in line gets granted. Pastor Jim's June board meeting provides an example. Brother Sack, the Boy Scout leader, presents a proposal for the church to buy tents and sleeping bags for the Boy Scouts. They all agree: "Sounds like a good idea. There is enough money in the bank. Let's do it."

In July, Deacon Donnie has an urgent request for money to repair a window that allows water to ruin the wall and floor below it. The board sees the need, but they are out of money.

Which is more important, the window or the sleeping bags? Without a budget no one decides. The rule is first come, first served. It would have been better to decide beforehand how much to spend for the building and for Boy Scouts.

Chapter 1 showed the need for a church mission statement. An outgrowth of a mission statement is church goals and then church strategies. A budget is a strategy to help a church meet its goals in order to fulfill its mission.

This leads to the next nonfinancial reason for budgets. After the church sets a budget program, leaders know exactly where they stand. The Boy Scout leader can plan his program within the Boy Scout budget, and the deacon can plan for building repair within his budget. Many churches give the program leaders a free hand in spending their budget. The Boy Scout leader and deacon do not have to bring specific requests to the board; they spend as they want just so long as they stay within their budgets.

At first this plan may worry some board members. They may doubt the scout leader's or deacon's judgment. But the overriding benefit is that the leaders enjoy the trust; the program's success or failure depends largely on them. Hence they will be more zealous and will work harder. A basic rule of management is to match responsibility with control. It is not fair to put a leader in charge of an area and not give that person power to act in that area. For instance, it is not fair to put the deacon in charge of the building and fail to allow him freedom to act.

WHAT ARE THE SPIRITUAL ASPECTS OF BUDGETING?

Jesus talked about the need for budgeting: "Suppose one of you wants to build a tower. Will he not first sit down and estimate the cost to see if he has enough money to complete it? For if he lays the foundation and is not able to finish it, everyone who sees it will ridicule him, saying, 'This fellow began to build and was not able to finish'" (Luke 14:28–30).

God wants us to know exactly what we are getting into when we follow him. The same advice applies to churches. Before we start a program, we must "estimate the cost."

The person in Jesus' parable estimates the cost to avoid public ridicule. The same principle applies to churches. A church that has money troubles is shameful. Those outside the church falsely use the church's money troubles as an excuse to reject Christ. They say, "All that church does is ask for money." If a church is careful about its budget, it can avoid this negative witness.

Some complain, "Where is faith in budgeting? Where is the Holy Spirit? Budgeting takes spiritual hopes and dreams,

removes the Spirit, and spits out cold, faithless numbers."
This is not true. Like a printing press, budgeting is a tool for
good or evil. The same press can publish the Bible and
pornography. Budgeting can be a cold, heartless number
machine, or it can amplify faith and the Spirit. The
spirituality of budgeting depends on the spirituality and the
wisdom of the people who control the budgeting. It is that
simple.

Church programs often come about like this: Someone,
perhaps the pastor, gets a flash of inspiration: "Let's start a
day care center for the elderly." At that moment the pastor
feels that the idea comes from the Holy Spirit and that the
Holy Spirit is completely involved in the project.

He sells the idea to the church. Then he plans and
budgets. By opening day, hours of work have gone into the
project. To lose the Spirit in the project is easy. It is no
longer God's project; it is the pastor's. The Holy Spirit
wants to work in every step of the process, not just the idea
stage. Why do we feel close to the Holy Spirit when we have
a good idea but not when we are budgeting? The Holy Spirit
is just as active in budgeting as he is in giving ideas.

There are other reasons why budgeting is important:
Budgeting reduces buying worries. If you are working
according to a plan, rethinking every purchase is not
necessary. Also, budgets guide members in giving. Members may not give if they lack a clear picture of the church's
needs.

A budget is a spiritual tool used to focus on a church's
purpose and direction.

MAKING A BUDGET

Children play a game where they stand at opposite sides
of the yard and throw a ball toward each other at the same
moment, trying to make the balls collide in mid-air.

Budgeting is like that. The budget committee tries to
bring together the church's income and the church's expenses like two colliding balls. There are three different
ways to bring together income and expenses. One way is to

estimate income and then budget expenses within the estimated income. Many companies budget this way. It makes sense.

Another way is to budget expenses and raise the income to cover the expenses. This process involves faith.

A third way is to start from both ends and meet in the middle. Have each department submit a budget, and also have a budget committee estimate income. Then hammer away at both ends until they meet.

The best way depends on your church. If your church is growing, eager, and prospering financially, budget expenses first and then raise the income. If the church is in financial trouble and members are not supporting existing programs, budget income first.

ESTIMATING INCOME

Estimating income is the most difficult part of developing a budget. It is also where churches spend the least time. There are several ways to do this.

One way is to get pledges from church members. There are both good and bad points about this process. First the bad; some people feel that pledges are contrary to the Scriptures:

> If you make a vow to the LORD your God, do not be slow to pay it, for the LORD your God will certainly demand it of you and you will be guilty of sin. But if you refrain from making a vow, you will not be guilty (Deut. 23:21–22).
>
> Again, you have heard that it was said to the people long ago, "Do not break your oath, but keep the oaths you have made to the Lord." But I tell you, Do not swear at all (Matt. 5:33–34).

Another drawback of pledges is that they may weaken your fund-raising ability. Getting pledges so you can make a budget is backward. Instead of enthusiastically buying into a church program, members think about money and its problems.

The good news is that pledges make your budget more dependable. Expenses are set at a more realistic level, and staying within budget is more likely. Getting pledges in advance is good in financially troubled churches.

Another way to estimate income is to look at last year's giving. Adjust it for inflation, changes in membership, and windfalls. Suppose last year's giving was $100,000. This is the starting point. Increase it perhaps 5 percent for inflation. Increase it 2 percent for membership increase, and remove the $10,000 that Brother Harris gave when he sold his store.

This method is realistic, but it ignores the members' giving ability and focuses on keeping the status quo within the church. It is the most commonly used method.

A third method has an interesting twist to it. It focuses on the church's giving power. Let's say the average family income for your community is $18,000. Your church is average; you have fifty families, so the members' total income is probably around $900,000. If every family gives 2 percent, the church income is about $18,000. If they give 5 percent, then church income is $45,000. Family income levels for your community are easily found in the census data in your library.

Combining the last two methods is a good starting point for estimating income. Adjust last year's income to get a minimum, estimate the church's giving power, then pray that the expenses fall between the two.

So far our focus has been only on finding income from gifts. This is not completely realistic since today's churches depend on other income sources. For example, many churches receive grants from the government or from foundations to do certain mission activities. Churches operate day care centers, meals on wheels, programs for the mentally impaired, and drug treatment centers. The government and groups such as the American Red Cross support these programs.[1]

[1]For more information on grants to churches, see Raymond B. Knudsen, *New Models for Financing the Local church,* 2d ed. (Wilton, Conn.: Morehouse Barlow, 1985).

ESTIMATING EXPENSES

A basic rule for budgeting expenses is to always base your cost estimates on what happened in the past. If you are budgeting for an existing program, figure out what it cost in the past. If you are starting a new program, phone around until you find another church doing a similar program and find out how they spend their money. Only as a last resort start out on your own; you will have to guess what the program needs and what it will cost.

This is what may happen if you "guestimate": You say, "If we start a day care center for the elderly, we will need a new phone, so I guess we had better add $30 a month to the budget. We will also need a part-time worker. We can probably get someone for $6 an hour. Six dollars times twenty hours times fifty weeks is $6000, so we need to add another $6000 to the budget."

There are two problems with this process: (1) You may miss thinking of something you need, and (2) things always cost more than you expect. In estimating cost for day care for the elderly, missing the cost of ramps and railings would be easy. Business phone lines cost more than $30 a month, and the $6000 budget for a helper ignores such things as payroll taxes and what to do when the helper is sick or on vacation.

A budget should not be made while sitting alone in your church office or working with a small budget committee. Include every possible member. Every person in any activity should give input. Start at the bottom and work up. Sunday school teachers discuss plans and needs with their classes, and the classes develop their priorities and new projects; estimating the cost. The Sunday school teachers go over their class plans with the Sunday school superintendent. The superintendent reviews the plans and costs and then goes over the entire Sunday school program with the pastor.

Every department needs to plan and develop a budget for its activities. The deacons focus on the building's needs. The youth leader meets with the youth. The missionary group sets its priorities. If this planning is done properly, program leaders will have a new sense of purpose and duty. Instead of the minister or a committee sitting in an office and coming up with a few new programs, there will be many new activities. Instead of the minister selling his ideas, the new programs already have member support.

Of course, the budget will be much higher if members create it, so you will also need to review the plans and their cost. Fund-raising is easier if there is a strong support base within the church. Every group must submit its plans and budgets to the budget committee. The committee must first have a clear report of what each group is planning to do.

Next the budget committee must decide if each budget request from each department is realistic. The budget committee's job is not to evaluate the programs. It simply is to decide if the budgets from the departments are complete and accurate. Suppose the youth department wants to start a Boy Scout troop. Their budget request lists one hundred dollars for a camporee. The budget committee does not evaluate the value of having a Boy Scout troop or of going to a camporee. It simply determines if the amount is adequate. It also decides if there are other items to include if the church decides to have a Boy Scout troop. The Boy Scout leader might overlook an expense, perhaps insurance.

Review all the budgets from the different groups in this way. Then go to the next step: prepare a minimum budget. This is the budget that keeps things running as in the past.

On another sheet prepare a wish list. It shows the new programs and the existing program's growth. It may look like this:

WISH LIST

Bibles for teen class	SS	$200
Boy Scout troop	Youth	1,000
New flooring for restrooms	Deacons	1,300
Increasing meals for Ladies Mission-ary Circle	LMC	1,800
Doubling literature distribution	Board	2,000
Increasing payroll	Board	5,000

Now the church must decide which programs it wants. It is important at this stage to get as much help in deciding as possible. Failing on this point destroys the entire budget process.

Setting priorities should not be done by a budget committee or a board. People support programs when they help make the decisions. The way you get everyone involved depends on your personal style. Pastor Jim publishes the wish list in the church bulletin and asks members to rank their choices. They turn in their ranking with their signature on the bottom. The next week the wish list is published in the bulletin with the vote tally. Pastor Jim also announces a church business meeting at which the final decisions are made.

At the business meeting Pastor Jim musters all his spiritual skills. He promotes some boring, but needed, items on the wish list. He explains that the members must accept or reject some programs as a package. The other items may be adopted in part. For example, they cannot buy Bibles for only part of the teen class, but they can scale down the literature purchase.

Everyone who wants to make a speech at the meeting makes one. Brother Ebenezer is in full bloom: "That floor in the restroom has been there for twenty years. It has worked fine all these years. Why waste good money?" Pastor Jim does not need to defend replacing the floor; it is not his idea. But since it is Deacon Donnie's idea, Donnie will probably speak for it. If Jim does talk in favor of it, no one can say Jim is just defending his own program.

Through the process everyone knows that the stewardship committee is going to ask for pledges to cover the new programs. Often generous members sponsor some new projects even before the church approves them. This can hurt the total church program if members reduce other giving to sponsor pet projects.

The initial budgeted income is not a limit in this decision-making process. The minister simply reminds the members that he will call on them to raise the money.

Churches often run into two problems after adopting a

budget. The most common problem is to go through the year ignoring the plans and the budget. The second danger is less common but more deadly: treating the budget as gospel. A church must always be flexible because unforeseen expenses arise and new opportunities open.

The entire budget process is hard work, but it is worth it because it is the church's primary planning tool and it inspires creativity and builds unity.

The next chapter reviews some more advanced ideas in budgeting.

8 | *MORE COST COUNTING: BUDGETS 102*

Every week Pastor Jim drives down the same country road to take his son to violin lessons. And every week he sees the same farmer driving the same Massy-Ferguson tractor in the same field. For weeks the Holy Spirit has been convicting Jim to stop and invite the farmer to church. This week he is going to do it. He is not as bold as he sounds. The farmer's wife has attended Pastor Jim's church for years. She is a real saint, and people also say good things about her husband. They say he is quiet and plain spoken.

A big-city minister develops guts to go visiting in the bad section of town, but it takes a special nerve to walk out across a field and start talking to a man driving a tractor. The farmer could just keep driving and leave Jim standing in the field all alone and feeling stupid. But, by God's grace, Jim has that special nerve.

Jim walks out across the field. He gauges where the tractor will be by the time he reaches it. He heads it off. As he walks up to the tractor, he gets a close look at Mr. Sturd. He is tall and skinny. It is easy to see that at one time he was very strong, but the years have left him hollow.

Mr. Sturd's hair is white now and his eyebrows are still black. His skin looks like tanned leather. His clothes are worn but clean. Honest sweat soaks his shirt. A bright red handkerchief is in his back pocket, and Jim can tell it has been doing duty wiping forehead sweat.

As Jim walks up to the tractor Mr. Sturd pulls to a stop

and climbs down. It is a strange few moments. Mr. Sturd does not appear very friendly, but Jim can tell that he does not mind the break. Mr. Sturd reaches behind his seat and pulls out a jar of water and says, "I'm sorry that I don't have a cup to offer you some. I wasn't expecting no company."

Jim says, "That's okay. I'm the pastor at your wife's church, and I've come to invite you to church this Sunday."

"I don't reckon I need to."

This catches Jim off guard. Must people he invites to church say they really have been planning to come and they really need to, but they just have not gotten around to it. Finally Jim says, "How do you figure you don't need to come to church?"

Mr. Sturd says, "Church is to teach you how to live better."

Jim mutters, "I guess that is . . . "

Sturd continues, "I don't need to go someplace to learn how to live better. I don't live as good as I know how now."

There is a long pause while Mr. Sturd stares at the sky. (Farmers spend a lot of time staring at the sky.) Finally Mr. Sturd takes a sweat-soaked pack of chewing tobacco out of his pocket. He opens his pocket knife and cuts off a piece for Jim. He says, "You're welcome to a piece if you chew."

Jim shakes his head no and says, "Thanks."

Mr. Sturd tucks the tobacco into his cheek.

Jim's mind races with a prayer. Out of the blue he says, "Would you teach me how to drive a tractor?" Mr. Sturd's face shows a faint smile. They spend the rest of the afternoon on Pastor Jim's tractor-driving lesson. He masters straight rows and smooth turns. Mr. Sturd does not say more than twenty words all afternoon, but somehow Jim feels welcome.

The next week Mr. Sturd is in church with his wife.

This chapter may hit many of you the same way church hit Mr. Sturd. Many of you may say, "I do not need another chapter on budgeting since I do not budget as well as I already know how." That may be true, but this chapter is full of information. No one should (or could) use everything in this chapter, but you may find one or two tricks to make your budget more useful.

Keep in mind that (1) budgeting is only a tool to be used in your church's total planning program; (2) you should plan your budget with help from as many members as possible; and (3) you must focus on programs, not on staying within some income level.

FLEXIBLE BUDGETS

In the last chapter we saw that members picked the programs they were willing to support, and then the stewardship committee raised the money to cover the programs. There is a weakness in this process in that members fail to link their giving with the church's programs. They vote for a program, but when it comes to paying for it, there is a strange detachment. They look at their own financial problems rather than the church's needs. Flexible budgets can help with this lack of support.

Prepare a few budgets. Five is a good number. The first is a bare-bone budget. It includes the minister's salary and money to pay the mortgage. The second budget includes things that may make life better, such as Sunday school lessons. The third budget is the same as the amount spent last year. The fourth budget is a moderate increase in spending with a few new programs. The fifth budget is the most hopeful; it includes many new programs. Use the first budget if giving is low. Use the other budgets when giving reaches certain levels.

If you are not certain of which budget to use, start with the first one, then use the second budget after you raise a certain amount. Kick in the third budget when you reach the next milestone, and continue in the same manner through the other budgets.

Another way to decide which budget to use is to go by the amount of pledges you receive. Get annual pledges from church members, and then reduce the total amount by allowing for those who do not keep their pledges. Choose the budget that fits within the pledges.

Flexible budgeting is safe, but it cripples church leaders in their planning. The youth leader worries whether the church will fund the youth retreat. The Ladies' Missionary Society becomes anxious about what to put on their calendar. Thus flexible budgeting should be used only in churches with money problems or in new churches without a history to help in planning.

PERPETUAL BUDGETS

Perpetual budgeting is done monthly. The budget for the month a year away is set at the end of every month. March 1991 passes. The board reviews the expenses for the month, then it makes a budget for March 1992. After April it goes through the same process for the next April.

At first perpetual budgeting sounds crazy, but it does have at least three good points. First, the church leaders are always planning. Second, since they review the budget every month, it is a living record and is kept up to date and sound. Third, the church works on a year planning horizon. When one month passes, the church adds another month to its plans. It is always planning a year in advance.

The drawback to perpetual budgeting is that it reduces input from all the members because you are not able to get broad input every month. Some members will ignore the budget. Also, when fewer members help with the budget, there is less innovation. The members at the monthly board meeting may get bored with it and thus fail to start new programs. Members not on the church board will not get a chance at innovation. It is easy for perpetual budgets to take a caretaker role with no surprises and no real innovation. Guard against this.

PROGRAM BUDGETING

The preceding chapter showed line item budgeting. Each line limits the expenses for the item, for example, "Yard care—$3,000." The line item budget focuses on expenses. Program budgeting, however, shifts the focus to programs. A budget might look like this:

Ministry within the church	
Christian training	$10,000
Pastoral care	50,000
Church services	3,000
Ministry within the area	
Community welfare	$5,000
Youth work	5,000
Ministry outside the area	
Home missions	$5,000
Foreign missions	10,000

Program budgeting is very logical. A church sets its goals, decides which programs achieve the goals, then gives money to those programs. The focus is on programs, not expenses.

Program budgets are the way church budgets should work, at least in theory, but sooner or later you must convert the program budget to a line item budget. Giving youth work five thousand dollars sounds good. However, sooner or later the treasurer will want to know how much can be spent by the Boy Scouts for tents.

Even though you must restate a program budget in useful terms, it is a good exercise for the church. What are the church's goals? What programs advance the goals? How much of the church's money goes to each program? How do the expenses advance the programs? Expenses should be considered last, not first.

Program budgeting makes fund-raising easier. Members react better to program budgets than to line item budgets. When Brother Collins looks at a line item budget, he looks first to see what the minister makes. Then he says, "Yard care—three thousand dollars! Boy, that's high! What can we do to lower this?" When he looks at the budget, he thinks of the church as expenses instead of programs. He thinks about his bills and decides that he cannot make a pledge. But show Brother Collins a program budget, and his response is better. He may say, "So this is what we spend on the kids? Is that all we do for outreach?" Do you see the difference?

CROSSWALK BUDGETS

Crosswalk budgets overcome the shortcomings of line item budgets and program budgets. Line item budgeting focuses on where the money is going, not on what the church is doing. Program budgeting focuses on what the church is doing, but it fails to show where the money is going. Crosswalk budgets combine the best from both.

Here is a simple crosswalk budget:

Fig. 8.1. Programs: Ministry within the church

Expenses	Total	Christian training	Pastoral care	Church services
Salary	$70,000	$20,000	$30,000	$20,000
Cleaning	10,000	5,000	2,000	3,000
Mortgage	30,000	15,000	3,000	12,000
Office	1,000	600	200	200
Literature	5,000	4,000	1,000	
Total	$116,000	$44,600	$36,200	$35,200

The top headings list the programs as a program budget would. The headings include all the church's programs, such as youth ministry and outreach. The side headings show the expenses like a line item budget. They include expenses such as water and cleaning. Of course a crosswalk budget for a real church would have more programs across the top and more expenses along the side.

The ideal way to fill in the figures on a crosswalk budget is to work from the bottom up. Start with the totals on the bottom, filling in what the church wants to spend on each program. This will set the money value the church places on each program. Then break the totals for each program into expenses. Add the expenses for each program to get the total for that expense.

This picture of crosswalk budgeting is ideal. A more workable way is to budget expenses and then divide them among the programs. For instance, set the budget for the electric bill, then divide it among the programs based on the area used by each program. Divide the total budget for salaries according to how workers spend their time. If 90 percent of the minister of education's time is in church training, 90 percent of that minister's salary goes under that program. Either way you do it, a crosswalk budget shows a unique view of the church.

ZERO-BASED BUDGETING

Most budgets simply modify last year's spending. We say things like, "Last year we spent $3,000 for repairs. Let's put $3,300 in the budget for this year." This makes sense. However, doing this for many years allows the church to wander away from its purpose. Programs are done not because they advance the church's goals, but because they always have been done. The church program becomes full of budgetary sacred cows.

Zero-based budgeting deals with this problem. President Carter made this type of budgeting popular in his attempt to balance the United States' budget. The idea is simple. Look at every expense and every program to see if it promotes the church's goals. There are to be no sacred cows. Cut every expense or program that does not advance the church's goals—even if "We have always done that."

History tells us about President Carter's failure with zero-based budgeting. He learned that there are many sacred cows in the United States budget, and he was powerless to do anything about them.

You may find yourself in the same place. Many items in your budget are firmly set by tradition, or you are stuck with certain expenses because of the church's commitments. You may start from a zero base, but you will quickly add in the salaries and the mortgage. You might end up exactly where you started.

Zero-based budgeting may dampen your spirit, because you will soon learn that neither you or the church board controls where most of the money goes. In any case, zero-based budgeting is a useful tool in a church bound by habits. It helps the members decide if they are exalting God or are just carried by momentum.

MANAGEMENT BY OBJECTIVE

Management by objective is a budgeting tool that combines strong management with the budgeting process. At the start of each year, the leaders of each program set their goals. Then a budget is made to help the program meet its goals. At year end the church rates a program using the goals set by the program.

The main focus is program goals. Good program goals have two features: they point to the church's overall goals, and they deal with actions, not outcome. A correctly stated goal for a Sunday school would be: "God willing, we will give out ten thousand handbills inviting people to Sunday school." This goal comes in line with the church's goals, and it focuses on action instead of outcome.

A poorly stated goal would be: "In 1993 the Sunday school will increase its membership by 20 percent." This sounds good and comes within the church's goals, but it is outcome focused. It misses how to bring about the increase. The apostle Paul said, "I planted the seed, Apollos watered it, but God made it grow" (1 Cor. 3:6). State goals in seed-planting or watering terms, not in growth terms. Growth is not our job.

Management by objectives is a good exercise. It focuses church members on what they need to do and helps them plan in solid action terms.

CASH BUDGETS

No matter what budgeting method you use, you should prepare a cash budget. A cash budget is made after you make your main budget. It shows when you are receiving and paying money. It shows you how much cash you need and when you are going to run out. Or if you have extra money, it shows how long you can tie it up in investments.

Church expenses are fairly constant from month to month, but giving is not constant. In many churches giving falls during the summer and is higher at year end. This means trouble for the church even if it has a good budget and is run within the budget. Money can easily run out, and cash budget shows when this will likely happen. Then you can plan for it either by borrowing or by moving expenses from lean months to fatter months.

Look at the budget for the Summerville Community Church:

Budgeted receipts	$25,300
Budgeted expenses	−23,900
Payments to denomination	−2,530
Other income	+2,400
Other expenses	−840
Net	$430

This looks like a good budget. The church pays 10 percent of its income to its denomination. The other income and expenses are from renting a house on the church property.

This budget looks okay until you see the cash budget (see fig. 8.1). The cash budget shows the money running out in August. There are two reasons for this. First, giving declines during the summer because members are out of town. Second, during the summer, expenses for this church increase because it gets hot in Summerville and so costs more to cool the church. The church also sends a few poor children to camp, the teens go to the beach, the minister travels, and the church has to pay the supply minister.

Cash budgets center on when the church receives or pays money. There is more to cash budgeting than dividing your budget by twelve. For example, notice the 10 percent

Fig. 8.2. Summerville Community Church cash budget for 1992

	Jan	Feb	Mar	Apr	May	Jun	Jul	Aug	Sep	Oct	Nov	Dec	
Beginning balance	1,000	1,080	1,110	1,140	1,170	1,100	640	180	(280)	60	460	950	
Budgeted contributions	2,000	2,000	2,000	2,000	1,900	1,900	1,900	1,900	2,300	2,400	2,500	2,500	25,300
Less													
Budgeted expenses	1,800	1,900	1,900	1,900	1,900	2,300	2,300	2,300	1,900	1,900	1,900	1,900	23,900
Payment to other organizations	250	200	200	200	200	190	190	190	190	230	240	250	2,530
Other budgeted													
Income	200	200	200	200	200	200	200	200	200	200	200	200	2,400
Payments	70	70	70	70	70	70	70	70	70	70	70	70	840
Balance at end of month	1,080	1,110	1,140	1,170	1,100	640	180	(280)	60	460	950	1,430	

payments to the denomination. April's receipts are two thousand dollars, so May's payment is two hundred dollars. There is a month's lag.

To solve their problem the Summerville Church simply waited until November to do some repairs. Churches with good budgets may still have cash flow problems. It is easiest to deal with cash flow problems if you catch them early. Cash budgets do this.

9 | A SPIRITUAL JOURNEY: FINANCES AND BUILDING A CHURCH

Pastor Jim eases down on the gas pedal as he heads out County Road 342. The speed limit is fifty-five, but he edges his car up to sixty. He is running behind schedule. The church is having a fund-raising campaign for a new church building, and visiting teams are out trying to raise money.

For the campaign Pastor Jim agreed to visit the church's older people. It seemed like a good idea because his evenings are tied up with church activities, and seniors generally prefer visits during the day.

Pastor Jim had planned on five visits this afternoon, but the last one had completely thrown him off schedule. It was wealthy Mrs. Grouse. Could she complain! First she told him about how her back was especially bad in damp weather; then she gave blow-by-blow details of her surgery; then she gave a complete run down on Sister Joyce's shenanigans and mentioned how her makeup is way too heavy, especially for a Women's Missionary Society president; and then she asked if he knew about Brother Hope's divorce back in 1967, and how . . .

At first Pastor Jim listened patiently, but Mrs. Grouse ran on and on. It came slowly at first. He tried stopping it by loosening his tie. Ten more minutes dragged by. He tried taking deep breaths. His eyes glazed over. He was suffocating—trapped at the bottom of a swirling pool of words. He gasped for air, but all he got was words. He frantically reached to pull himself out, but the words pushed him deeper and deeper. Finally with one desperate last kick he forced his way out. He does not remember what he said or how he did it, but at last he was free and breathing in the cool late afternoon air as he headed out of town on County Road 342.

Mrs. Grouse had ruined Pastor Jim's afternoon in two ways: she wasted several hours and completely dampened his spirit. His first impulse was to go home and have a big bowl of ice cream (his moral equivalent to a stiff drink), but he decided to go on. Almost like a cowboy being thrown from a bronco, he knows that he must make the next visit. He knows that if he goes home now it will be weeks before he musters enough courage to go visiting again.

Pastor Jim's next visit is with the Widow Cherish. He makes the turn onto the dirt drive that leads to her house. Daffodils grow along her drive. They have been there for years, and each year they have grown thicker and thicker. Pastor Jim pulls up to her house. Even though it is nearing dusk, he can see that the yard is neat though it shows its age. Farm equipment neatly parked in the old shed sits quietly rusting. A weathered wooden glider is under an old oak, and a dark green porch swing sways restlessly in the early evening breeze.

Jim goes to the back door. He usually goes to the front door, because people expect that of a minister, but at this house the back door seems right. The screens on the back porch are covered with plastic, forming a makeshift hothouse. He gently taps the door, almost afraid to disturb the silence.

The porch light comes on, and the Widow Cherish looks out the window and flashes a large grin. She opens the door and a cat ambles out and rubs against Pastor Jim's legs. She says, "I'm glad to see you. It gets mighty lonely out here in these woods. Come on in. Let me fix you some pie. You'll have some pie, won't you?"

"I'd love some," Jim says, "but I can't eat it now. I hate ruining my supper. I haven't eaten since lunch."

Sister Cherish's wrinkles break into an even bigger smile. "That is the best news I've heard all day. You need to sit yourself down and have supper with me. It'll only take a minute. I never have anybody to eat with. Especially no one as well educated as you. This'll be a real treat."

"I really can't. I'm sure my wife is expecting me for dinner. What were you thinking of having anyway?"

"Well, let's see. I have some creamed corn and pole beans, and I'm cooking up a mess of collards and some biscuits. I can be ready in twenty minutes."

"Maybe I can call Janet and see what she thinks."

During dinner they talk about the book of Romans and how tasty fresh corn is. She tells him where her husband's favorite fishing hole was and how to plant tomatoes so the cutworms cannot get them. After dinner Jim helps her dry the dishes and puts them in the cabinets made with the same tongue-and-groove paneling used in the rest of the kitchen. He says, "I hate eating and running, but if I don't get home, Janet will kill me."

"Well, aren't you going to talk about what you came to see me about?"

"What was that?"

"Well, last week in church you said people would be visiting the members about giving to the new building."

"I was having such a good time that I completely forgot. Anyway, I hate bothering you about it. I know you must have a hard time making ends meet."

Widow Cherish gave Jim her only frown. She said, "No, I've already decided what I can do to help. When my husband died in 1957 I got five hundred dollars from his insurance. I cashed the check and hid the money in a fruit jar under a loose board in the bathroom. I've been saving it for a rainy day. Every June 17 I get it out and look at it to make sure that it is okay. June 17 is the day he died. Come help me get it."

In the bathroom, Widow Cherish pulls the string that turns on the bare bulb above the basin and kneels down and pries up a loose board between the toilet and cast iron bathtub. She removes a jar. Inside are five crumpled one-hundred-dollar bills. She takes them out and squeezes them into Pastor Jim's hand and says, "John would've liked knowing these were building a church."

Jim's throat swells up inside. His watery eyes look down at the old money and a smile plays on his lips. At first he thinks about protesting, but then he says, "Could I come out for dinner next week? I'll bring some groceries."

"That would be wonderful. I've been wanting some peach cobbler. Why don't you bring some vanilla ice cream!"

As Jim pulls out on County Road 342, he thinks that somehow this evening made his job worthwhile.

The real danger with a book of this sort is to convert the basically spiritual process of giving into cold calculations and fund-raising strategies. A chapter on fund-raising for a building could easily rob the process of its heart. We must not fail to recognize that the whole fund-raising process belongs to God. Money comes as God moves on the hearts of church members and bankers. Money for church buildings comes from three places: money the church saves, money the church raises, and money the church borrows.

MONEY SAVED

Arriving at the amount of money your church has saved may be more difficult than you think. A good starting point is the church's surplus cash, although each month surplus cash waxes and wanes. Spring and fall giving is higher, and expenses may be uneven during the year. May's cash surplus might just get you by for the summer. A cash budget will show this.

After you have a firm figure for cash surplus, you still must adjust it. Set aside a crisis reserve. Every church should squirrel away cash equal to a few months' expenses to help cover such surprises as the breakdown of the furnace, a member's home burning, or general hard times that reduce giving.

RAISING MONEY

There are many ways that churches raise money for buildings. They range from bazaars to weekly promotions, from poster board thermometers to mystery days.

No matter how you run them, all good campaigns have a few features in common: good goals; focusing on people and needs, not buildings; one-to-one visits; and a payment time period.

Goal Setting

A fund-raising campaign needs two goals. One is a basic goal of building a fine building. The second is a dream goal of building a larger building or improving its quality.

Goal setting is difficult. Start by looking at your regular giving. A church can easily raise the same as one year's regular giving. Often churches set goals twice the annual giving. Many churches raise five or six times that level.

Does regular giving go down during a fund-raising campaign? Amazingly, regular giving often goes up during a capital campaign. People like giving when they see something going on and when they feel a part of the action.

The Focus Is People and Needs

A campaign does not need complete plans or building sketches before it can start. The focus is not building a building; it is meeting church needs—not "What a pretty building this will be!" but "Our church fills up every week. We need more seating or we will have to start turning people away."

One-to-One Visits

Visits spawn giving. They help members become part of the plans and show them how their involvement affects the project's success. A church service appeal cannot do this.

Get advice from the members you visit. They may have some helpful input. After all, the building will serve the very people you are visiting. When they feel involved in the project, they will give more freely.

You should make a direct request to each member, asking him or her to prayerfully consider a pledge. Leave the member a pledge card and ask him or her to turn it in even if no pledge is made. This will help you keep track of visits and determine who is still thinking about the pledge and who has made a decision. It also will make the member face the decision. Otherwise many members will not make a decision but will set the pledge card aside, planning to think about it later.

Before leaving pray for the project and the home.

The pastor need not do all the visiting; other church leaders should help. Fund-raising is easier when it involves more people.

A Payment Time Period

In many respects, the shorter the campaign the better. Week after week of fanfare is smoke in the members' eyes. The church size and the visiting teams control the length of the campaign. It may last only a few weeks.

No matter how long the campaign, the actual payment period should be several years long. Only a few people save money, and those who do earmark it for something special. Committing future income is easier.

Will the members honor their pledges? Usually the amount pledged comes in. The members making the pledges pay only about 80 or 90 percent of their pledges; this shortfall is made up by some paying more and by others who will not make pledges giving anyway. This good result comes with nurturing and nudging those who make pledges. This may include reminders in church bulletins and writing letters to thank donors whenever they make a payment or when they reach certain milestones in their giving. For example, when members pay half of their pledge, write notes thanking them for their sacrifice.

Fund-Raising Things to Do

1. Start raising money a year or two before construction.

2. Print a brochure. Include a building summary (the

focus is the details of the needs, not the paint color or the siding), a description of the financial plans, and the campaign details (goals, visits, dates, etc.).

3. Print pledge cards. They should say something like this: "Thank you for your pledge. Please return your pledge card even if you cannot make a pledge right now. This will help us keep track of visits. All pledges are confidential."

4. Find leaders who will help visit. Include as many program leaders as possible. Training should include a prayer session to ask God for blessings and wisdom as you visit. It also should include a complete briefing on the building, featuring church needs, not the actual building details. Get the leaders to "sell" the building every chance they get, not just when they are visiting. This will make the actual visiting much easier. Also explain the pledge cards and have some mock visits.

5. Have the visiting teams divide up the church members using some scheme they like. They may divide the visits according to where people live, or they may select people they know.

6. A few weeks before the campaign, announce the campaign in the bulletin and church paper.

7. Kick off the campaign. Hand out pledge cards and brochures during the worship service. Give a brief talk on the needs the building will meet and give a sermon on the collection for the tabernacle. Tell the members that a team will visit them to explain the building details.

8. Each week print and announce the total pledges to date.

9. After the visiting, host a breakfast for your teams. Avoid comments like "This is a victory celebration!" Simply invite the teams and thank them for their hard work.

10. Every quarter write the members to remind and thank them for their pledges. Update them on the building's progress. Invite those who did not make a pledge to get on the bandwagon. Many churches keep at least one visiting team active seeing new members.

With all these details, neglecting spiritual things is easy. A fund-raising campaign is best when Christ and his sacrifice are woven into every activity. Focus on prayer and make your visits spiritual times of building God's kingdom. The building program will succeed if the giving is Spirit led.

There is a list of rules for visitation teams that reads like a list of school yard rules. Do not pit one team against another. No one knows which team is the best. Keep all pledges confidential. (Even the pastor does not need to know. It is amazing how much giving is an attempt to please the pastor.) Printing the donor list works fine for a museum, but not for a church. Avoid celebrations that build ungodly pride; plan a thanksgiving meal instead. Avoid anything that allows you or the members to take God's glory.

BORROWING MONEY

Unlike the Bible models, most churches borrow money for major building projects. There may be spiritual problems with debt. Even today Solomon's wise words still ring: "The rich rule over the poor, and the borrower is servant to the lender" (Prov. 22:7). Many churches are built debt free. The church must decide if it should borrow. Raising all the money is possible.

There are many ways churches can borrow. One way is to borrow from members. The interest rates banks charge are a few percentage points higher than rates they pay depositors. Members may earn 7 percent interest on certificates of deposit, and the bank charges 10 percent interest on mortgage loans. If the church borrows from its members at 9 percent, everyone is better off, except the bank.

To borrow from church members using a changing rate is a good plan. This rate can be based on a certain number of percentage points above the prime lending rate. Another way to borrow from church members is to borrow over short periods, perhaps five years. After five years everyone involved can decide if he or she will go for another five years. A member may bail out, or the church may get a regular bank loan.

Suppose you borrow $100,000 from members at 1

percent less than the bank would charge, and you do this for only five years. It still would save you $5,000.

Some denominations borrow from their members in a big way. The members loan money to a fund, and the fund loans money to churches. Usually everyone profits. It pays the members a higher interest rate than the banks, and it charges the churches a lower interest rate than the banks. Members can withdraw their money when they need it without hurting the program. All the members share the risk, so no one is badly hurt when a church fails to make its payments.

How Much Can We Borrow?

Whether you borrow from the members or banks, borrow only a safe amount. Borrowing too much disheartens church members and hurts other church programs. It also may snowball and restrict growth. Skittish members may move to other churches, so fewer people share the burden, so more members move, and so on. Finally the faithful remnant must give up. This further insults God. People drive by the vacant church building and wag their heads, and the bank curses its loss. Everybody loses because the church borrowed too much.

Following are some guidelines that may help you decide how much to borrow.

1. Debt payments should use only 20 percent of the church's annual total receipts. This includes all receipts, even those that go to the denomination. How do you determine the loan payments? Imagine a thirty-year, 12-percent interest rate loan. Payments will be $100 a month for every $10,000 borrowed.

2. Do not borrow more than 50 percent of the total cost of the building. Most banks will not loan more than this, because selling a church is difficult.

3. Keep payments below what the church has shown it can save.

Warning! Many churches discover that they do not meet the bank's loan rules. For example, the bank may loan only 60 percent of the building cost. The church would like

Fig. 9.1. Loan payment and interest cost chart
on a $100,000 loan at 12 percent

| Length of loan | Payment | Principal balance after: | | | Total interest cost |
		5 Years	10 Years	15 Years	
5	$2,224	-0-	-0-	-0-	$33,440
10	1,434	$64,497	-0-	-0-	72,080
15	1,200	83,652	$53,953	-0-	116,000
20	1,100	91,774	76,746	$49,500	164,000
25	1,053	95,653	87,756	73,410	215,900
30	1,028	97,663	93,417	85,705	270,000

to borrow 80 percent. The church borrows the shortfall from its members, bypassing a safety switch the bank uses to protect itself and the church. Do not finagle ways to bypass the bank's rules.

For How Long Should We Borrow the Money?

The shorter the duration of the loan, the better. Figure 9.1 shows a 12 percent, $100,000 loan. It shows the payment and interest cost for various loan lengths.

If you reduce the popular thirty-year payback period to twenty years, your payment will increase by $72. However, your total interest cost for the church will go down $106,000. If you reduce a twenty-year debt to fifteen years, your payments will increase by $100, but your total interest cost will be lowered by about $50,000. So keep the payback period twenty years or less.

How to Apply for a Loan

The church should make a neat and professional prospectus that gives the lender an overview of the church. Include anything that will convince the bank that the church can repay the loan. Include these things:

        Background details
            Brief church history
            The area's demographic details
                Population
                Income levels
                Population growth

        Building details
            Architect's plans
            Building site photograph
            Plat showing the building on the land
            Appraiser's recent land appraisal
            Builder's or architect's total cost estimate

        Financial details
            Graph that shows giving over past years
            Church financial statements for the past few years
            Church budget

Credit history (including all present and previous creditor's names and addresses)
Report showing the money members have raised so far

The fellowship
Graph showing church growth
Church members' names and addresses
Church leaders and their church and nonchurch jobs

Make several copies of your prospectus. Have a local print shop bind them into professional-looking booklets. Now go shopping.

In the past people used one bank for their entire lives. But times have changed. There is often a big difference in interest rates between banks. Imagine a $100,000, twenty-year loan. Lowering the interest rate 1 percent will lower the loan payments $70 per month, or $17,000 over the life of the loan. It pays to shop for the lowest interest rate even though it involves some work.

Interest rate shopping can be confusing. Banks pull many tricks to make it look like they are giving a lower interest rate. For example, they charge points. These are payments made to the bank at the beginning of the loan. They are really additional interest costs. They have many other tricks that are too numerous and too complex to explain here. If you lack experience, find someone who has it. There likely is a church member who can help, or the church may hire a CPA to help pick out the best loan. The couple of hundred dollars it costs to hire a CPA may save thousands.

When dealing with a bank be professional and positive. Do not focus on the collateral backing up a loan, but show that the church can repay the loan. When someone does not repay a loan it counts as a bank error. This is true even if the bank can foreclose and recoup all its money. Showing good collateral is not as vital as showing that you can repay the loan.

People or churches that are in desperate need of money are not the bank's favorite customers (nor do they get the best deal). Dire need may indicate a lack of careful planning.

Bankers want a well-thought-out growth plan. They like to see the bank as part of a bigger plan.

This chapter focused on fund-raising in a cold, clinical way, but do not forget how this chapter started: money comes as God moves hearts.

10 | SURVIVAL: A CHURCH BUILDING PROGRAM

It is a great day, a terrific day! Surely this is the day that the Lord has made! Nothing can make it better. Pastor Jim is ecstatic. No, even ecstatic is too weak a word.

Finally, after months of planning, hours of work sessions, repeated prayers, member gripe sessions, and a few fights with architects and builders, it is done—finally, complete, and absolutely done. Well, almost. The men's room is missing a few tiles, and the choir loft lights blink when someone flushes the women's room toilet. The building is done, and today is the first service in the new church.

You would think Jim had just birthed a baby. Months ago he started calling the church building "she." When someone asked how the building was coming, he would say, "She is coming along fine." Or if there was a problem, "Her wiring is having trouble." In one sense she was closer than his own children. After all, the past few months had been hers.

Jim thinks this is his crowning feat. He sings praises to God for his protection during the process. There were so many traps, so many pitfalls, so many decisions. Without God's care it would have been a disaster.

This book is not meant to distract from God's working. Nothing that a church does affects its long-term well-being like building, so a pastor should not start a building program unless he has proof that God is blessing. Unless a church can kneel and get God's leadership, it should forget building.

Perhaps an example will drive this point home. One question always raises its nasty head: "How big of a church do you want?" This question leads to two imponderables: "What will be the church growth over the next few years?" and "How much can we borrow?" What a paradox! If you have growth, you can borrow more. If you borrow more, you can build a larger church, and that may foster growth.

Many church buildings swallow their members. Their leaders had a growth vision that did not come true. Their pews are empty, and their debt smothers them. On the other hand, many churches must rebuild within a few years because they outgrew their new buildings.

Choosing the right building size affects the church for years. Formulas and rules of thumb can help, but nothing can replace God's help.

BIBLICAL BUILDING PROGRAMS

The Bible shows four major building examples: the tabernacle, Solomon's temple, Zerubbabel's temple, and Nehemiah's wall.

The Tabernacle

The wilderness tabernacle building program was a pastor's dream come true. Just imagine God giving Moses the exact design and sizes. After all, the sanctuary was "a copy of the true one" (Heb. 9:24). It was a reminder of God's redeeming work. Our church buildings must reflect that same purpose.

Imagine God moving the people to give. The gifts were so abundant that Moses had to send some people away. God blessed Bezalel and named him the contractor. God described the furnishing and outlined the dedication ceremony. What could be better?

Solomon's Temple

Another Bible building project is Solomon's temple. David wanted to build the temple, but God gave him another job—to secure Israel's peace (see 2 Sam. 7:10; 1 Kings 5:3). Since David could not build, he smoothed the way for his heir. There are many lessons here.

Before you build, seek peace within the church. Building a church is the most stressful thing a church can do. It is the small things that cause trouble. Members decide on the design in ten minutes and then argue for weeks about the nursery's carpet. Some ministers think that building a church will unify the members, but that is wishful thinking. Start a building program only after you are sure that the church is peaceful. David's job may be yours. God may want you to secure peace within the church so that the next pastor can do the actual building.

The building of Solomon's temple teaches us other lessons, too. He used the best material, and it was costly. He used gold weighing 7,500,000 pounds and silver weighing 75,000,000 pounds. Today the gold would be worth $62,400,000,000 and the silver worth $9 billion.[1] All this in a fairly small building! Astonishing!

Building plans always involve trade-offs. For example, using the best carpet makes sense. Quality carpet lasts longer and makes a spiritual statement: "Nothing is too good for God." On the other hand, being frugal makes sense: "Save the money and use it in soulwinning." Surely you need the Lord's help in making such decisions.

The building of Solomon's temple teaches another lesson. The workmen cut and dressed the stones a hundred miles away: "No hammer, chisel or any other iron tool was heard at the temple site while it was being built" (1 Kings 6:7). This is similar to the lumberyard cutting all the wood and you merely fitting it together. This does not mean that modern churches must be built like this, but it does show the detailed planning that went into God's building.

---

[1] This is figured at $390 per troy ounce for the gold and $5.60 per troy ounce for the silver.

Zerubbabel's Temple and Nehemiah's Wall

All pastors dream that their building program will go like Moses's tabernacle and Solomon's temple, but realism shows us Zerubbabel's temple and Nehemiah's wall. Everything that could go wrong went wrong: first, they had to deal with government red tape (see Ezra 1; Nehemiah 2); then outsiders worked to destroy the project and tried to discourage the workers and upset the plans. The builders were so intimidated that they built with one hand and held a sword in the other (Ezra 4; Nehemiah 4). The members faced one spiritual crisis after another (Ezra 10; Nehemiah 9). Look for your building program to be more like Ezra and Nehemiah's than Moses and Solomon's.

RENTING A BUILDING

The previous section presented two important lessons. Build only after these are in place. Does the church trust God's leading? And is there peace in the church? If not, back off and settle these two issues.

Sometimes there are other reasons to put off building. A few more growing years may unite the members, or the construction of a new freeway may open cheaper land. In the meantime, you may need to consider alternatives to building.

You can rent a school, theater, retail space, or a church. Renting retail space is a good idea because it gives the church more exposure than a school. Some areas have many vacant stores, and owners enjoy having a church pay rent. You might find a vacant church building or rent from another church and hold afternoon meetings. Many Seventh-day Adventist churches, which meet on Saturday, rent their churches for Sunday services. You may even want to rent or buy a modular church. These are like double-wide mobile homes with a steeple of sorts. They make good classroom space if that is what you need. Of course all these ideas are only short term, but they may buy you time.

You might not want to rent, but this does not mean that you have to build; buying a church may do the trick.

BUYING A CHURCH VERSUS BUILDING

Before you build, do a complete search for an existing building. Look for vacant churches and for other types of buildings that could be converted. An old warehouse or school may work. If you find an occupied church that you think may meet your need, call the pastor; the present congregation may be outgrowing the church and planning to move on.

Buying a used church has both good and bad points. On the positive side, buying a used church is cheaper than building a new one. There are not many buyers for used churches, so they lose their market value quickly. Used churches often sell for less than they cost. Some congregations will sell their building for less if they know that another church will take good care of it. Often, used churches and major overhauls are cheaper than new churches.

Another positive aspect of buying an existing building is that the cost is firm. When you buy a church you know what it will cost; not so when you build. Also, when you buy you can see what you are getting. Architect's sketches lack realism. A blueprint is not the same as walking through a church's rooms. Although the building may have some problems, they may not be as bad as ones hidden in a set of blueprints.

Buying a used church is not trouble free, but it does involve fewer hassles than building your own church.

ORGANIZING A BUILDING PROGRAM

Pastor Jim likes to talk about the fun he had building the church. "We had our planning meetings on the first Tuesday night of each month. We always tried to have a meal. I learned a long time ago not to try to get the saints to make a decision on empty stomachs. Hungry people can be downright hard to deal with. While people were eating I would kick the meeting off with a short devotion and prayer."

Whenever Jim tells this story he likes to lean back and prop his feet up. "After the prayer, we had a joint decision-team meeting. Early in the project we just talked about a general vision for the building or about each decision team's job. Later we used the joint meeting for decision team reports."

A decision team is Jim's catchy term for subcommittees. He uses the name *decision teams* because that is exactly what he wants them to be. To him, subcommittees bring reports; decision teams make decisions. Any church member may serve on any decision team.

"After the joint meeting we broke into nine decision teams. One was trying to decide what land to buy. Another was looking for an architect to use. You get the idea.

"The church appearance team was choosing colors and drapes—that sort of thing—when a big ruckus broke out. We hadn't even bought the land or hired an architect, and they were arguing about what color to paint the sanctuary. I went into the room, and both Sister Clovis and Brother Harnon were holding color charts that they had picked up on their way to the meeting. She had a Hune's Lumber color chart and he had a Gamble's Hardware color chart.

"Well, you're not going to believe this, but they both picked out the exact same color—same color, just different names. One was peach blossom, and the other was . . . I can't think of its name—something about a flower.

"Anyway, they were arguing. I acted like Solomon and said, 'Show me the colors, and I'll help you decide.' I studied one. Then I studied the other. I couldn't tell them apart. They were the same color! What a trap! Everyone was watching me squirm, expecting me to settle this war. You know, 'Blessed are the peacemakers,' and all that.

"Then came this sudden rush of an idea. I give God all the credit for it. I simply said: 'They both look pretty to me. Either one will do.' Then I left. They went back to arguing for a while and then came to what they called 'a compromise.' How can you compromise between two colors that are the same?

"That was not the only weird thing that happened when we were building the church. Once this dog walked in while the builders were there and. . . ."

A Game Plan

Pastor Jim's story teaches us that we need a game plan. Table 10.1 is a general list of the tasks you need to do when building. A detailed list would be several yards long. Also, this list's order is not doctrine. For example, the earlier you hire an architect, the better. Having an architect to help you pick out land and plan it is a real comfort.

Table 10.1. Some tasks in building a church

Determine the church size you want.

> Study your church's growth data.
> Study your area's growth data.
> Study your church's desires for more programs.
> Convert all this studying to a desired church size.

Determine the church size you can afford.

> Study past giving patterns.
> Have a fund-raising program.
> Project giving.
> Decide how much to borrow.
> Prepare a loan request.
> Shop for a loan.
> Apply for a loan.
> Close the loan.

Determine the size and other needs for the programs using—

> Sanctuary
> Classroom space
> Kitchen
> Church offices
> Fellowship hall
> Library
> Church music area
> Play areas

Nursery
Restrooms
(Note that the focus is program needs, not building design.)

Buy the land.

Determine the amount of land you need.
Find the land.
Bargain for the land.
Engage a lawyer to do a title search.
Close the land deal.

Obtain the final plans for the building.

Search for an architect.
Bargain over architect fees.
Sign the architect's contract.
Tell the architect everything learned so far.
Work with the architect to get good plans.
Help the architect make final plans and specifications.
(This includes choosing building materials and fixtures.)

Build.

Obtain builders' bids.
Select the builder.
Balance cost and quality.
Buy insurance before building begins.
Oversee building.

Landscape.

Hire a landscape architect.
Hire someone to do the work.

Move in.

As you look over the list, it is easy to see that you will not be able to do everything yourself. First, there is just not enough time; and second, if you make all the decisions yourself, you will make people angry. So get plenty of people involved.

Committees can be a way to save time if you do not feel like you need to go to every meeting. Members must be taught how to work to an end rather than just sitting there churning. Committees also provide you with more ideas than you would come up with alone. And they build broader support than if you decided things yourself.

Some pastors like to build and want to work on everything. Others see building as a necessary evil and would rather focus on their outreach programs. Some pastors like a central decision-making group; others enjoy managing subcommittees. Take a close inward look before you set up your building program.

Besides looking inwardly, study your church. Some churches like central power; others spread out power. Some think that everything should be done by the members, and others think it is best to hire people. There are several good ways to set up a building program, so carefully tailor your plan to your church.

Three jobs should be done when you are setting up your project's structure.

First, carefully lay out your job. Then write job descriptions for the key positions.

Second, decide who has the power to act. Can the building committee decide what land to buy or should that decision be made by the church board or perhaps even the entire membership?

Suppose the plumber is standing there with two types of faucets for the restroom. Does the architect or the minister tell him which to use? Or does this decision need to go to the appearance team, the building committee, the church board, or the entire church?

Third, members get involved when they feel a part, and they feel a part of things they work on, so get the members working on as many things as you can.

Take a note pad and spend a day on a nature hike. You and God can decide the best way to set up your building program.

Pastor Jim's Structure

Pastor Jim's story gave a clue about his structure. Jim took on the role of "coordinator." He figured that since the members were going to have to pay for the building and to use it after he was gone, they ought to decide what to do.

Therefore he did not want to work on every decision. He saw his job as finding conflicts between one group's plans and another and helping the groups to resolve the conflicts. For example, the appearance team chose office furniture for the pastor's office while the structure team included some built-in furniture. Jim closely followed both groups and spotted the problem right away.

After Pastor Jim figured out what job he wanted, it was easier to do the rest. He searched the membership roster and found a member who showed a strong leadership. He asked her to lead the building committee. At first Joyce objected, "I don't know anything about building."

Jim gave Joyce a gentle push. "What counts is leadership. There are several good builders in the church. They know how to build, but they lack the skills to bring us through the whole process." So Joyce agreed.

After some talk, Jim and Joyce decided to set up several decision teams. Any member could join any decision team. They recruited certain people to head certain decision teams. The teams would make decisions and report to the general building committee which was made up of all the decision-team members.

Decision teams

Here are Joyce and Jim's decision teams. Except for the last, they are shown in the order in which they started work:

1. *Church growth*. This team studies such things as past church growth and census data for the area. Then it estimates church growth. The finance team and the plans team need this guess to help them decide how big a church to build.

2. *Land*. This team defines what the land needs are. Based on the demographic data and projections done by the church-growth team, it finds the land. It then negotiates the price. This team needs to know the city, county, and state codes for church buildings. Try to find a Realtor to be a team member.

3. *Program*. This team defines the program needs for the auditorium, the kitchen, the classroom space, office space,

church music room, etc. It finds out exactly what building design the church needs. The program team's work feeds the plans team.

For example, the program team studies the current kitchen and carefully reviews its use in big functions such as church dinners and weddings. It also reviews its small uses, for instance, the day care center storage of milk and sack lunches. The program team talks to the church members to see how they would like to use the kitchen. Using all this information, the program team says something like, "The church needs a kitchen to prepare dinner for two hundred people. It should also have a large walk-in cooler to serve the day care center." It does not specify exactly how the needs are to be met; it just gives the needs to the plans team. The program team may break down into smaller teams to check into each church program.

4. *Finance team*. This team controls the money for the entire project. It helps decide how big a church to build. It plans fund raising and borrowing, and it approves all building fund payments.

5. *Plans team*. This team has two functions. First, it searches for and hires an architect. Then it works to make the plans by pulling together the program needs, the financial limits, and the growth data into blueprints.

6. *Building team*. This team takes bids and hires and deals with the builders. Members must know something about building.

7. *Furnishings and appearance*. This team uses information from the program and planning teams. It decides what furniture to buy and makes decisions about appearance, paint color, drapes, etc.

8. *Landscaping*. This team plans the landscaping. This may include hiring a landscape architect, approving plans, and hiring someone to supply and plant the grass and shrubbery. Do not forget this team, especially when you are doing your budget. A new church without decent landscaping is bleak.

9. *Legal team*. The legal team oversees the project's legal aspects. During a building program a church signs several

contracts—to buy land, borrow money, and hire architects and builders. The legal team approves all these contracts and helps the church to follow denominational rules.

The legal team also oversees the insurance during the building program. A church needs protection against mishaps on the building site and a policy for fire and other dangers during building. It may need architect and builder's performance bonds.

Do not neglect to develop this team, thinking that insurance is the builder's duty. Someone who gets hurt on the building site will likely sue the church. If fire destroys the unfinished building, it is the church's loss. It may be the builder's fault, but the builder may not have enough money to cover the loss, leaving the church with nothing.

If the church does not have a member who is a lawyer to serve on this team, hire one. It is the best money you can spend.

There are many ways to organize your workers. Organize them in the best way for you and your church, and God will bless you in this process.

11 | OX MUZZLING: WORKERS AND PAY

Before the meeting a cool evening shower converted the blistering hot day to a welcome seventy degrees. The first part of the board meeting went well. Pastor Jim carefully minded his P's and Q's because he knew what was on the agenda for the meeting's last half. Once a year it happens— his salary review. The board will ask him to leave the room.

Brother Ebenezer will talk bad about him: "He sure knows how to waste time in meetings." He always says that.

Old Miss Dulcet will say something good, but untrue, about him: "He is one of the finest young men I have ever known, and he has such a sweet wife and adorable children." She always says that.

Then Brother Ebenezer will roll his eyes back and shake his head: "He sure knows how to waste time in meetings." He always does that. It is the same every year.

Pastor Jim leaves the building into the cool night air. The crickets chirp and every so often a lightning bug flashes. He walks toward his car but decides to walk home. It is less than a mile, and he can use some head–clearing time. He walks down Elm Street's slight incline and begins praying.

"Dear God. It has been a long time since I've had a raise. I'm broke. The car is dying. The washing machine is broken. Janet hates taking the clothes to the laundromat. I guess she has talked to you about that already. Things sure aren't going very well for me down here. Are you sure you want me to be a preacher?"

Pastor Jim walks along in the silence. Some kids play hopscotch under a street light, and a distant dog barks. A cool breeze hits his face. Jim does not get his answer that night.

MUZZLING THE OX

Since Genesis, paying the preacher has been a problem. Genesis 14:20 says that Abraham gave the priest Melchizedek a tenth of the spoils from thwarting Kedorlaomer. Moses taught in Deuteronomy 14:28–29 and 26:12 that the Levites get the tithe, but Israel soon quit paying tithes. This forced Moses's grandson, Jonathan, to wander about looking for a home (Judg. 18–19).

Pastors' pay was an early church concern. The apostle Paul wrote,

> Who serves as a soldier at his own expense? Who plants a vineyard and does not eat of its grapes? Who tends a flock and does not drink of the milk? Do I say this merely from a human point of view? Doesn't the Law say the same thing? For it is written in the Law of Moses: "Do not muzzle an ox while it is treading out the grain." Is it about oxen that God is concerned? Surely he says this for us, doesn't he? Yes, this was written for us, because when the plowman plows and the thresher threshes, they ought to do so in the hope of sharing in the harvest. If we have sown spiritual seed among you, is it too much if we reap a material harvest from you? If others have this right of support from you, shouldn't we have it all the more?
>
> But we did not use this right. On the contrary, we put up with anything rather than hinder the gospel of Christ (1 Cor. 9:7–12).

Paul's feelings are common today. There are four good ideas in these verses. First, support of the pastor is the church's duty. Pastors should not have to work other jobs to supply their needs. Second, supporting a pastor is a good deal for the members. The pastor sows spiritual seeds, and all that is due back is a material harvest. Third, support is a pastor's right. It is not something a church does out of kindness or compassion, but out of duty. Fourth, at least to Paul, the Gospel is more urgent than the right to support.

In this section we will look at setting the pastor's pay. The things covered here also apply to church workers. We will look at four pay systems: the ability-to-pay system, the market system, the need system, and the reward system.

THE ABILITY-TO-PAY SYSTEM

The ability-to-pay system is the most common pay scheme, and it is also the worst for everyone concerned. It first looks at all the other budget items. It then gives the pastor any money that is left over. If estimates of the church's income and the budget is tight, the first thing cut is the pastor's raise.

This system is not logical because it forces the pastor to avoid outreach since any added cost will hurt him and his family. And since church budget pressures are normal, the pastor's pay is forced to follow behind other expenses' growth. After awhile the underpaid pastor gets discouraged and quits. The church, used to getting by with underpaying the pastor, hires a new one. But the new pastor costs more than the old and this causes a money crisis. The crisis may even look like the new pastor's fault, and this new pressure will cause more problems.

It is much better to set the pastor's pay by using some other system and plugging it into the budget and paying him just like you do the electric company or mortgage holder.

Embryonic churches may need the ability-to-pay system for a while, but the members and pastor should have some plan to fix the inequity it causes.

THE MARKET SYSTEM

Describing this system is easier than using it. The goal of this system is to pay the pastor the same as other people in similar settings. What do people with the same schooling, experience, drive, and duties get paid? To find out, send surveys to or phone area pastors and ask them what they make. Also ask them about their education, experience, and duties. Contact seminaries and ask them what their graduates are making. Or go to the library and look up government documents listing pay for ministers. Finding a job description that matches your pastor's, and setting his salary to match the one you find, appears simple, but there is a big problem.

The problem comes from comparing diverse people and jobs. People are unique, jobs are unique, and comparisons are tough. For example, consider schooling. When you are setting your pastor's salary, do you look at other people with theology master's degrees? How about social science master's degrees? Or do you look at people without master's degrees? After all, ministerial master degrees do not help someone get a nonchurch job.

Look at experience. Suppose your pastor finished school ten years ago. Should you average the pay of all pastors who have ten years since school, or should you pay the same as new graduates receive? Some churches pay new graduates more than older pastors. This is called salary compression and is caused by the ability-to-pay system.

Even if your church does not use the market system, it should do an area-wide check to insure that its pay is not too far off.

NEEDS SYSTEM

In the past, churches set pay by using a needs system. This system says that a pastor is working for God and that the church must meet the pastor's needs. The "muzzling the ox" verses come into play here. A pastor's needs are to be met by the people served; other rewards come from God. The idea is still common today. Workers for many ministries today (i.e. Campus Crusade) must raise their "support." The focus is on covering the worker's needs.

A few pastors were asked, "What do you think should go into setting a pastor's pay?" They all replied based on need: "The church should pay for a pastor's children's private school tuition." "The church should provide a parsonage." "The church should pay for the pastor's phone." "Pastors with more kids should get paid more."

Bible teaching and church history support this, but it is an odd system. In nonchurch jobs most people's pay connects to some output. A store clerk makes five dollars an hour since this is the clerk's market value, and he or she produces work that is worth more than five dollars an hour for the store. The clerk's rent, number of children, and the children's school cost do not enter into setting pay.

More problems arise if the pay system focuses on the pastor's needs. Pastors with the same needs should be paid the same, and pastors with different needs should be paid differently; so younger pastors with many children should be paid more than older pastors with larger churches.

A final problem with the needs system is sorting needs from luxuries. There are people alive today who can recall when cars or phones were luxuries. You likely remember when such things as clothes dryers, microwave ovens, and dishwashers were only for the rich. Now the modern family "needs" these things. Who makes the decision whether something is a need or a luxury? Are pastors allowed any luxuries? As society changes and "needs" change, is staying up with the latest "need" the church's job?

Although the needs system is firmly Bible backed, it does have problems. It is awkward for churches and pastors in that the pastor must sell the church the needs and the church must decide if the pastor is truly needy or just a poor money manager.

REWARD SYSTEM

"Be careful not to do your 'acts of righteousness' before men, to be seen by them. If you do, you will have no reward from your Father in heaven" (Matt. 6:1, 4). The final reward for our efforts is spiritual. Pastors and laymen alike should always "run in such a way as to get the prize . . . a crown that will last forever" (1 Cor. 9:24–25). However, a church cannot expect its pastor to work solely for a spiritual reward.

In the same place Paul connects spiritual seed planting and
material harvest: "If we have sown spiritual seed among
you, is it too much if we reap a material harvest from you?"
(1 Cor. 9:11). There is a link between action and material
rewards. Figure 11.1 shows a pastor's reward matrix.

	GOOD	BAD
SPIRITUAL	Pat on back Saved souls Healed families Affirmation Pay raise Etc.	Griping members Arguing board Moving memberships Etc.
MATERIAL	Pay Raises Parsonage Car Etc.	Pay cut Sell the parsonage "Fines" Etc.

Fig 11.1. Pastor's reward matrix

The group labeled "spiritual" broadly uses this term. It
embraces all the pastor's psychological needs.

Research shows that punishment destroys a worker's
willingness to work. Punishment may result in a short-term
output increase, but in the long term it will hurt output.
Removing the "bad" elements is a way a church board can
enhance the pastor's well-being. Shielding the pastor from
your church's Brother Ebenezers may give a greater reward
than a 20-percent pay increase. Protecting the pastor from
church board battles may be worth as much as doubling the
pay.

There are many myths about material rewards. For
example: "Pay a person more and he or she will be happier";
"I can improve workers' output by rewarding more output
with more pay"; "If I pay a person enough, I can treat that
person any way I want"; "Problems cause unhappy
workers. Fix the problems, and you will have happy
workers and more output"; and vice-versa, "Something

causes happy workers. Take it away, and you will have unhappy workers with lower output."

This last myth sounds like a riddle. But consider an absorbing theory by Frederick Herzberg. He calls it the motivator-hygiene theory. The theory says jobs must have certain things, and workers are unhappy if they are missing. He calls these things hygiene factors. Hygiene factors do not cause a person to work harder. They merely keep the person from being unhappy and leaving. On the other hand, motivators increase a person's output. Take away a motivator, and the person will not be unhappy; he or she will just not do as much. Figure 11.2 shows Herzberg's two factors.[1]

Hygiene Factors	Motivating Factors
Company policies	Feeling of accomplishment
Pay	Feelings of achievement
Benefits	Recognition
Supervision	Personal growth
Working conditions	
Job security	

Fig. 11.2. Herzberg's two factors

If research supports this two-factor system in the secular work setting, how much more should it stand in a church? How can churches sanctify this theory so they can use it in setting the pastor's pay? The Bible plays down the hygiene factors and focuses on the motivating factors (except recognition). Hygiene factors deal with money and other material benefits. On the other hand, there is nothing that motivates like the feeling of accomplishment from seeing a soul led to Christ.

Using money as a carrot to get a pastor to do more does not work. A plan that says, "We will give you a thousand-dollar raise for every fifty new members," will not prod a pastor to work for new members.

Often money is a way to give recognition. Recognition

---

[1]For a complete discussion of Frederick Herzberg, see Craig Pinder's *Work Motivation* (Greenview, Ill.: Scott Foresman, 1984).

is a motivating factor. Suppose Jim has a satisfactory salary. He works hard, and this pleases the church board, who gives him a raise. He does not work harder on account of it, but the recognition afforded by the raise may result in more work.

Good pay may cause content pastors, but it will not inspire them to do more. The board should make sure the hygiene factors are in place, but they should not think anything will happen until the motivating factors are there.

LINKING THE SYSTEMS

All the systems reviewed had some good points, except the most common, the ability-to-pay system. Your church's pay system should choose the best from each system, set the pastor's pay, and raise the money to cover it. Use the following steps.

1. Take the starting pay and adjust it for inflation. Figure 11.3 gives the Consumer Price Index since 1980. Multiply this starting pay times the current CPI and divide the product by the CPI when hired. This is an inflation-adjusted starting salary. The pastor should be making more than this.

Fig. 11.3. Consumer Price Index

(1982–83 = 100)

1980	82.4	1985	107.6
1981	90.9	1986	109.6
1983	96.5	1987	113.6
1984	103.9	1988	118.3

(Source: U.S. Department of Labor, Bureau of Economic Statistics)

2. Review the changing needs in the pastor's family. Adjust the result of step 1 for these need changes. Add, perhaps, $1,500 for household additions. Add another $2,000 for each college student. Do not reduce it for a spouse working outside the home.

Steps 1 and 2 estimate the pastor's starting market value adjusted for inflation and changing needs.

3. Ask other churches what they pay their pastor. Be careful to compare similar jobs.

4. Contact the seminaries that service your church and ask them what this year's five top graduates receive. Average their pay.

5. Contact your local mental health clinic or other social service agency. Ask what someone with your pastor's service years is making. (This is public information.)

Pay the pastor at least the amounts found in steps 1 through 4. That is, pastors should make more than their starting pay altered for inflation and changing needs and at least as much as other pastors, social workers, and seminary graduates.

After finding the lowest logical pay, adjust it to reward for zeal, output, continuing education, church growth, etc.

The church should not stop there. It should disarm anything that will distract from a helpful climate for the pastor. It should also build in motivators such as affirmation, sense of accomplishment, and personal growth. This can do more than raises.

TAXES AND EMPLOYEES

Chapter 5 talked about the church's tax-exempt status, taxes, and giving. This section looks at employee tax problems. The problems that go with the earlier topics are being compared with the employee tax problems. Making errors in this area is easy and results in high fines, sometimes even higher than the amount of tax you owe. More people are jailed for tampering with employee taxes than for income tax fraud. This happens when employers withhold taxes from employees' paychecks and fail to give the withholding to the Internal Revenue Service. The employer is acting as the IRS's agent, and if the employer sidetracks the money, it is clearly fraud. This is not the same as deducting an expense that may not truly be deductible. Be careful handling employee taxes.

Employee or Not an Employee?

From the tax side, life is much easier if a person working at the church is not an employee. If a person working at the church is some corporation's employee, you do not do anything about his or her taxes. If a person working at the church is self-employed, and you have paid that person more than six hundred dollars during the year, you must fill out Form 1099 at year end. This form shows the person's name, address, social security number, and the amount the church paid. Give the self-employed worker a copy and send the IRS a copy. The self-employed worker must handle all the taxes.

How do you decide if the worker is an employee or is self-employed? Treating workers who are employees as if they are self-employed can cause many problems. For example, if a church makes this mistake, the church must pay all the worker's social security tax and a big fine. The court uses these guidelines to determine if a person is self-employed.

1. Does the worker set the work hours?

2. Does the worker decide how the job is done? The church can define the job and set standards, but the self-employed worker decided how to do the job.

3. Is pay based on hours worked or the finished job?

4. Does the worker do this job for people other than the church?

5. Is the job done at the church, or is it done at the worker's home or business?

6. Does the worker own the tools, or does the church provide them.

7. Is the job often done by self-employed workers (e.g., roofing), or is it usually done by employees (e.g., office workers)?

8. Does the worker have many diverse duties or just one task?

9. Does the worker carry a liability policy usually carried by a self-employed person?

A church typist who works from nine to five under the

pastor's direction is an employee. But if the pastor gives handwritten drafts to someone who does typing at home for two dollars a page, this person is not an employee.

If the church hires someone for general repair work around the church, this person is an employee. But if the church hires someone just to replace the roof, this person is probably self-employed.

A housekeeper working set hours and using the church's supplies is an employee. Someone cleaning the church sometime during the week and working undirected is likely self-employed.

If the church is contracting out jobs such as repairs and cleaning, it should make sure the person or company hired has adequate liability insurance and dishonesty bonds. These policies protect the church from paying for mishaps.

Temporaries

Hiring "temporaries" is a way to avoid the employee tax and liability problems. The yellow pages list temporaries under employment contractors. The church pays the firm, the firm pays the worker, and the firm worries about taxes, insurance, etc. Smaller churches that do not need a full-time person can benefit from temporaries.

It is a shame if you hire someone who quits a job to work for you and then you decide you cannot afford that person. With a temporary, if you find that you cannot afford him or her, you simply call the agency and they assign the worker to another job. Also, if the work runs out half way through the day, you must keep an employee busy, but you can send a temporary home.

Temporaries can be hired for most church jobs: janitors, handy persons, office workers, and kitchen help. The firm handles interviewing, hiring, and firing. They also keep time sheets, prepare paychecks, and do the tax chores. They pay payroll taxes and buy workman's compensation insurance, liability insurance, and dishonesty bonds. These services are not free, so a church should count the cost and see if it is worth dodging these headaches.

Hiring Members

A member loses her job, and the church rescues her as the church typist. A mill worker gets laid off, and the church hires him to do some minor repairs. The church must look after its members. However, hiring members is risky business. It hinders normal employee/employer relations. Reproof is more difficult, and minor problems with the member/employee's work may become intense. Also, the worker probably will not talk about problems, and malice will build. You could have a real mess if you had to fire a member/employee.

Hiring a member/office worker is uniquely troublesome. This member will know all the church's business. All the pastor's plans, troubles, etc., will pass under the member's nose, possibly hampering pastoral planning and counseling.

On the other side, hiring a nonmember broadens the church's exposure, brings news ideas, and advances the office's professionalism.

Taxes

Having paid workers is made complex by the red tape of taxes. There are many detailed regulations to follow and severe fines for failing to follow them. (See appendix 4 for tax forms.) IRS *Circular E* details the tax rules. Here are some of the high points:

1. New workers must fill out a W-4 form. The W-4 shows how many allowances a worker claims. Step 2 uses this information.

2. At the end of the pay period, you must figure each employee's gross pay. This usually is the hourly rate times the hours worked.

3. Determine the federal withholding tax by using the *Circular E* tables. First find the tables for the pay period: weekly, biweekly, semimonthly, monthly, etc. Then find the table for the employee's marital status (single or married). Look for the employee's pay and allowances. Then

find the withholding amount. States with income taxes use the same type of tables for state withholding.

4. Next determine the amount to withhold for social security taxes. At the time of writing, this is 7.51 percent of the gross pay. Do not withhold this tax on any pay that exceeds $48,000. These two figures go up every year, so get the latest rate from the current *Circular E*.

5. Write the paycheck for the gross pay minus the federal, social security, and state withholding taxes.

6. Tax deposits usually are made by the next month's fifteenth day. For example, you would deposit June's withholding by July 15. A deposit is done just like a bank deposit except it goes into the IRS's account. Add all the month's social security taxes, and then double the amount. Add the month's federal withholding taxes and write a check for the total. Fill out Form 8109. Give a bank teller the check and Form 8109 and you are done.

You must double the social security because the employer matches what the employee pays. Suppose you withhold $15 from an employee's paycheck for social security and $10 for federal income tax. You need to deposit $40—15 plus 15 plus 10.

7. At the end of the quarter fill out Form 941. This form reports all the withholding and social security for the quarter and the payments made. For the January, February, and March quarter, mail Form 941 by April 30; for the April, May, June quarter mail Form 941 by July 31; and so forth.

8. Fill out W-2 Forms for your employees at year end. They are due by January 31. Give them to the employee, and send the IRS a copy along with Form W-3. Form W-3 simply recaps all of the church's W-2s.

These forms and deadlines are almost overwhelming, but the whole process is simple after you learn it. Perhaps someone in your church who has employees will help you. If not, the clerk at the IRS will review procedures and make sure you are doing things right. If your church has many employees, hire a bookkeeping service to handle payroll.

12 | *COMPUTERS: A NECESSARY EVIL?*

Now I must tell you a sad story—the story of Pastor Jim nearly losing his job. A few years ago Pastor Jim was very disheartened with his ministry. He poured out his woe to his wife, Janet: "Brother Ebenezer is acting up. Giving is down. It has been months since my last baptism. And I have so many things to do: I haven't written my sermon, I haven't done the bulletin, and I need to work on next year's budget. What I need is a computer!

"I could use it in writing my sermons, the bulletin would be a snap, and I hear they have programs that budgets fall out of. The church could use it for bookkeeping, too. I could use it for keeping track of members. I could use it for raising money—for writing personal letters and all that stuff. We could put our interest file in it and keep track of visitors. You know, a computer could be a real soul-winning tool. It would be great."

Janet said, "Didn't Gus Gorden say he was buying a new computer and that he was selling his old one? Why don't you give him a call and see what he wants for it."

Pastor Jim called, and Gus said that he would give his old computer to the church. Jim was so excited that he went over right away and picked it up. He came home beaming: "He gave me copies of all his software, too. There's word processing, a spreadsheet, and a thing called BASIC. I can do anything with all this stuff."

Pastor Jim cleared his study's desk and got right to

work. This is when the trouble began. The computer grabbed Jim. He was hooked. Addicted. Compulsed. For weeks he did nothing but work on that computer. Janet worried about him—he hardly ate. He quit visiting, and he would spend only a few hours working on his sermon. He yelled at the children.

People would ask Jim what he was doing, and he would say "I am writing this program to keep track of members." Or, "Watch this—all I do is input hymn numbers and the bulletin prints itself."

Whenever anyone would suggest that Jim may have a problem, he denied it. "I am doing this for the church. This is part of my ministry. I have this program that sends visitors a card. This will really improve the church's outreach."

Jim's addiction continued for weeks until finally the church board dealt with the problem. Brother Ebenezer made a speech about this being the straw that breaks the camel's back. He said Pastor Jim needed to be fired. No one agreed with Brother Ebenezer, but everyone did agree that something needed to be done.

Finally, Gus Gorden spoke up: "I'll take back the computer. We can lock it in the church and only let him use it, say, two hours a day." Everyone agreed that this was a good idea and went home. The plan did work, and Jim kept his job.

This story is not as extreme as it at first sounds; actually it happens quite often. Why does this happen? In many ways a pastor's job lacks clear feedback. After a day of visiting the sick, writing sermons, dealing with church problems, and witnessing, it is sometimes hard to answer the question, "What have I done today?"

Computers, by contrast, provide concrete results with quick feedback on success and failure. This can serve as a real tonic to harried pastors. It works like other hobbies such as photography and shortwave radio. The problem is that since computers can be so useful in the church, pastors sometimes use them as a sham retreat from their real calling.

Pastors who get computer fever must do frequent self-testing. "Is this truly helping the church? What is the eternal fruit of my labor? What if I'm doing computer work and someone with a soul need knocks on my study door? Will I gladly stop what I am doing, or will I resent the holdup?"

This chapter's purpose is to acquaint you with computers. This is difficult for at least two reasons. First, some of you know nothing about computers, while others could easily write this chapter. Second, computer products are rushing at us at mach speed. New products will blast some of this chapter to the land where the world is flat, the sun travels around the earth, and phrenology is a major pastime.

SHOULD THE CHURCH BUY A COMPUTER?

Yes. In the past, this chapter would have discussed how churches weigh the pros and cons of buying a computer, but recent years have seen computer prices fall. Now a church can get some computer setups for less than a thousand dollars. Even small churches can justify this cost for its help with the sermon, church newsletter, bulletin, letter writing, and membership list. Many pastors find that they would rather have a word processor than a part-time typist.

WHAT TO BUY?

A computer system has two parts: hardware and software. Hardware is the equipment. Software is the electronic commands that control the computer. Choose hardware and software together. If you buy the wrong hardware, it might not run the software you decide you need. If you select the software first, it may not run on the hardware that you can afford.

HARDWARE

A computer system has four basic hardware elements: the computer itself, the keyboard, the monitor, and the printer. Usually the computer and the keyboard come together.

Computer and Keyboard

Two types of computers have emerged after years of development—those that focus on graphics, such as the Macintosh, and those that focus on data, such as the IBM. Actually both machines can do about the same things. Learning the Mac is easier, but it costs more. Newsletters can be made on the Mac with ease, but it might not run the church accounting program. There is less software for it, and it costs more. At this moment only the Apple computer company produces the Macs. Others are trying to clone it but have failed—so far.

On the other hand, there are many IBM-type machines, and they are less expensive. Each one is slightly different from the others. Sometimes the manufacturers build in special features to make their computers attractive to consumers, but they cut corners. Just because a computer claims to be "IBM compatible" does not mean that it will run your IBM-type software. Make sure that the software you want runs on the computer you want before you buy it. Make sure that it appears on the screen the way it should and works at the speed it should.

You also must decide how much memory you need. Memory is the amount of data the computer can hold at one time. Each software package has an amount that it needs. If you do not have it, it will not run. Memory comes in bytes. A byte can recall one letter or number. All you need for most software is 640,000 bytes, or a 640k memory (*k* stands for thousand).

You also must select the computer's mass storage device. The mass storage device saves programs, data files, and other output from the computer until you need them. The computer will save them in your mass storage device when you tell it to. For instance, you may use a word processing program to write a letter. When you are writing the letter it may be in the computer's memory, but you must save it on a disk before you shut the computer off.

The two mass storage options are floppy disk and hard disk. They both record data like cassette tapes record music.

Floppy disks are square envelopes that cover a round disk. The computer reads the disk through a slit in the envelope. You insert it into the computer whenever you want it read. Most floppy disks hold about 360,000 bytes (360k). A more recent floppy style holds twice as much. This chapter uses about 30k memory. One 360k floppy disk will easily hold this entire book.

Hard disks work the same way as floppies, except they are hard and mount inside the computer. Hard drives hold much more than floppies. A common size is 40,000,000 bytes. In computerese that is 40 megs. So a 40-meg hard drive holds the same as 110 floppies, or 110 books this size. Buying a hard drive cuts out the need for many floppies.

Buying a hard disk is a good thing, but hard disk drives do have their problems. First, they sometimes break down, and when they do everything on them is lost. Guard your hard disk by often backing it up on floppy disks. Fortunately, special programs compress the data so that you do not need 110 floppies to back up your data. The hardest part is remembering to do it, but just as soon as you neglect it, the machine breaks down and all is lost.

Another problem with hard disks is many users. Unless they are careful, many users can clutter up a hard disk so badly that no one knows good files from bad files. Also, there is a security problem. If you save a letter on the hard disk, anyone who uses the hard disk can read it.

Many churches keep the computer programs on hard disk and keep data on floppies. Floppies also crash, but at least backup is easier and not as much is lost if you lose one floppy. Some people file floppies with their hard copy so that when they are working on a project the disk is right there in the folder.

Monitors

Monitors are a little easier to understand. When buying one you must consider the size, color versus monochrome, and image quality. Buying a television is simple: the bigger the better, and of course you want color. But monitors are different. When you use them for many hours, a good quality image on a monochrome screen is better than poor image on a color screen.

The number of light points or pixels, in a given screen space set the image quality. The more pixels in a given space the better. Monitors must also work with the computer, so before you buy a monitor, make sure your computer can use it.

Printers

The church's printer selection may be more important than the computer. There are four printer types: daisy wheel, dot matrix, ink jet, and laser.

Daisy Wheel Printers. Daisy wheel printers have a wheel that looks like a tiny wagon wheel without the outer rim. The dozens of spokes are like rays coming from a center axle. Each spoke's outermost end has a letter shaped on it. When the computer tells it to print a certain letter, it spins to that letter, a little hammer taps the spoke against the printer ribbon, and the letter is printed.

Daisy wheels print good quality characters, and are the least expensive good quality printers. There is no major cost after the initial outlay. On the other hand, they will not print graphics, such as newsletter titles and headings. They are very slow and noisy.

Dot Matrix Printers. Dot matrix printers have an array of pins which an electric magnet pushes out instantly. To make a letter, the magnet pushes out the correct pins that shape the letter. The pins hit the printer ribbon, shaping the letters on the paper. Better quality printers have more pins, and they produce better letter quality by reprinting each letter. The paper slightly shifts for the second printing, and the pins fill in the white space between the dots already on the paper.

Dot matrix printers are the least expensive type of printer and can print near perfect letter quality. However, photo copies of dot matrix printed material are poor. Dot matrix printers are faster than daisy wheel printers and can print graphics. They also have no major cost after the purchase.

Ink Jet Printers. Ink jet printers form letters by squirting ink on the paper. They are faster than daisy wheel and dot matrix printers and give very high quality text and graphics printing.

Operating costs for ink jet printers are very high. Before you buy, check the per page ink font's cost. They easily break down, and repairs are costly.

Laser Printer. In laser printers the printer memory composes a page and then projects the page on a metal drum using a laser beam. The drum is electrostatically charged where light touches it, so powder clings to it like lint clings to a wool shirt. The charged drum rubs against black powder, and the powder sticks to the drum only where the laser light charged it. Then the drum is run against paper which picks up the powder. Finally the printer bakes the powder on.

Laser printers give the best quality text and graphics printing. They are faster and quieter than most other printers and are more expensive. Operating costs are about the same as running a photocopier. They are reliable, but when they break down repairs are expensive.

SOFTWARE

Software is the electronic commands that make the computer do what it is supposed to do. Software divides into four groups: operating systems, utilities, general programs, and special programs.

Operating Systems

The operating system is the computer program that controls the computer's workings. It tells the disk drives how to save data, it oversees the memory use, and it controls the data flow to the processor.

Operating systems are one area in which you have no choice about software. They come with whatever machine you buy. However, you need to learn to use your operating system. For instance, you will use it to copy files from one drive to another. Getting a good grip on your operating system is necessary for obtaining the most from your computer.

Utilities

Utilities are programs that help you run your computer. They do things like recovering lost files or backing up your hard disk. "Memory resident programs" are a special utilities group. They stay in memory, running at a certain key's touch. They do things while you run a program. For example, one such program checks your spelling as you type from the keyboard. It pings whenever you misspell a word. Touch a certain key and a thesaurus pops up synonyms. Utilities are handy tools.

General Programs

General programs are useful most everywhere. The major types are word processing, spreadsheets, and database programs.

Word Processing. A pastor's life is words: praying, studying the Bible, developing sermons, writing newsletters, making visits, and counseling. A good portion is written and a word processor makes the written part much easier. It allows a pastor to type letters, sermons, and study notes; save them; edit them; merge them; and finally print them. Every pastor should own a word processor.

A special type of word processor is a desk-top publishing program. Pastor Jim uses it to do layouts and to choose special fonts that give bulletins and newsletters a typeset look.

Spreadsheet Programs. Spreadsheet programs are the workhorses for people who handle finances. They are to numbers what word processors are to words. An example explains what they do best. Picture a budget worksheet. The budget is for the church expenses for each of the twelve months. The worksheet has the names of the expenses down the left column. Each row shows some expense. The names of the months are at the tops of twelve columns that run across the page. "Cells" are where rows and columns meet. For example, there is a cell where the water expense row crosses the February column.

The computer can do math with the cells' numbers. It can add, forming row and column totals. It can graph the growing expenses. You can use it to change one cell's value to see how it changes the total financial picture. It can do statistical studies, and it can sort by size. The list goes on and on. But churches hardly do such things. So even if the church makes a complex budget once a year, it is hardly worth the effort to stay skillful for that once-a-year chore. Spreadsheets should go at the bottom of your computer wish list. Perhaps a member who is active in spreadsheets can put your annual budget on one for you.

Databases. After a word processor, the church needs a database program. A database program keeps track of certain data fields for each record. For example, a database package for a church may be set up to keep a record for each member. You can keep track of each member's address, map coordinates, job, birth date, attendance record, and last pastoral visit date. These would each be set up as database fields, so for each record (member) you have this data.

Once it is set up, you can sort and print this data for each member. For example, you can sort by birthday and print a list that shows every January 1 birthday, every January 2 birthday, and so on. This makes sending cards on members' birthdays easy.

You can sort by zip code and print address labels, sort by the date of the last pastoral visit to see who needs a visit, sort by map coordinates so that you can visit by area, and sort by church job to see who does what.

Many special church programs try to give you these same features, but they lack a decent database program's flexibility. You can also use database programs in other jobs besides member records. They can track equipment, church interest, and school enrollments to name a few.

Special Programs

Special programs are programs that serve a special need. For example, church programs can track giving, make receipts, keep a membership roster, and record music. What they do can usually be done with a good word processor and database manager, and they often cost a lot for what they do. They may look good but be very inflexible. You may spend hours getting used to running the membership list program and then find that the same program cannot work for church school enrollments. A general database manager does both, so avoid special programs.

There is one exception. A church of over 150 members should put its accounting on a computer. It needs a program that records gifts, makes receipts, prints and records checks, and records funds. General accounting packages do not work with funds, so you need an accounting package made for churches.

There are a few good accounting programs for churches available. Choosing the one that is right for your church can be tough. Look at how well it matches what you are doing by hand. How difficult is entering data? How complete are the instruction books? How flexible are the reports it produces? How many giving families can it handle? How many gifts can it handle? Can it handle budgets and budget comparisons? Who do you know who has success with the program? How easy is setting it up to run? And, finally, how good is the software support? An always busy toll-free number is no help.

Two Final Notes About Software

When you look at new software cost, remember the set-up cost and the learning cost. Usually the personnel cost of setting up and learning new software is more than the initial software cost.

Also, using commercial software that you did not pay for is unethical. Illegal software copies are flooding Christendom, but using an illegal copy is as wrong as shoplifting. It is not right to do it just because "everyone else" is doing it.

CONCLUSION

Sometimes when people read a book like this, they miss the trees for looking at the forest. This section reviews the high points of each chapter and gives you another chance to think about how to apply them in your church.

Chapter 1 looked at the need for planning, organizing, directing, and controlling in the church. Every church program should include these points.

Chapter 2 discussed the spiritual role of the church treasurer. The job is guided and empowered by the Holy Spirit. It also looked at the traits a treasurer should have.

Chapter 3 looked at the need for separating the church's record-keeping jobs from cash control.

Chapter 4 showed a sample record-keeping system and how to do a bank reconciliation.

Chapter 5 listed the three criteria for deducting a gift on your tax return. A gift must be to a qualified organization, there must not be a direct benefit to the donor, and there must be no strings attached. This chapter also looked at trusts as a good fund-raising tool for churches.

Chapter 6 showed that certain property gifts may cost the giver much less than it at first appears. The chapter also showed the tax forms a church needs to send to the IRS when it receives large property gifts.

Chapter 7, the first budget chapter, focused on the need to get as many members as possible helping in the budget process. It showed budgeting as a bottom-to-top process.

Chapter 8, the second budgeting chapter, looked at a few alternative budgeting tools.

Chapter 9 covered raising money to build a church. It looked at fund-raising and debt. It showed fund-raising as a spiritual process.

Chapter 10 focused on organizing church building programs.

Chapter 11 talked about setting minister's pay and the problems churches face when dealing with employee taxes.

Chapter 12 reviewed computer hardware and software.

PASTOR JIM

You may be curious about whatever happened to Pastor Jim. A few years ago he left the ministry to sell water softeners. He nearly starved. He now calls this time his sabbatical. After much prayer and against the opposition of Brother Ebenezer, his old church rehired him. Oddly, at the board meeting where the rehiring of Pastor Jim was discussed, Brother Ebenezer stood up and pounded his hand on the table and said, "You'll hire him over my dead body." At that point Brother Ebenezer had a mild heart attack. Since then Pastor Jim has visited him several times in the hospital, and things seem to be on the mend.

APPENDIX 1
INTERNAL CONTROL CHECKLIST

This is a list of ideal internal control features for churches. Usually, the larger the church, the more of these you use. However, do not think that just because you have a small church you can neglect internal control.

General

1. A church should have a blanket bond that insures against members or employees stealing.
2. Everyone involved in handling and accounting for cash should change jobs in the church every so often.

Cash Receipts

1. Centralize cash receiving activities in a few hands.
2. Persons receiving cash should have no access to accounting records.
3. Deposit cash receipts quickly.
4. Instruct the church's bank to not cash checks made payable to the church.
5. Distribute contributor's receipts promptly after month's end.
6. Forbid check cashing from cash receipts.

Cash Payments

1. All payments other than petty cash should be made by check.
2. Require two signatures on checks.

3. Prenumber all checks.
4. Do not sign checks in advance.
5. Support all payments by bills that:
    a. Show that the goods were received.
    b. Are approved for payment by the person responsible for that fund.
    c. Have accurate math.
    d. Are canceled so as to prevent double payment.
6. Someone other than the person writing the checks should promptly reconcile the bank statement.
7. Keep an imprest petty cash fund. An imprest petty cash fund works like this: Establish a petty cash fund for say fifty dollars. This is done by cashing a check for fifty dollars. Put the fifty dollars in a box. Each time a payment is made out of the fund, the receipt is put in the box. So if the church gives the mail carrier five dollars, a five-dollar receipt is put in the box with the money. The box always has money and receipts totaling fifty dollars. When the cash in the box gets low, cash a check that is equal to the receipts in the box, and use this cash to replace the receipts in the box, again making a total of fifty dollars in cash in the box.

Fixed Assets

1. Keep detailed property records.
2. Make periodic inventories of fixed assets.

Accounts Payable and Purchasing

1. Use prenumbered purchase orders.
2. Check invoices from suppliers for accuracy.
3. Maintain an approved list of vendors.
4. Compare suppliers' monthly statements with recorded liabilities.
5. Take advantage of all cash discounts. Passing up cash terms of 2/10 net 30 is equal to paying 36 percent interest.

Payroll

Independently check the payroll.

APPENDIX 2
BANK RECONCILIATIONS

Doing a bank reconciliation, or "balancing the bank," is a job that is simple if you know how to do it but difficult if you do not. A bank reconciliation is done to find out if your checking account balance is the same as the bank's balance.

Why is this done? For one thing, it finds bank errors. Because banks deal with a great number of checks every day, mistakes are inevitable.

A bank reconciliation also finds mistakes in your records. Suppose you write an incorrect amount down in your checkbook or copy into your journal incorrectly. The easiest way to find the mistake in your checkbook or journal is to balance the bank.

Balancing the bank also provides internal control over the cash (chap. 3).

Before going through reconciliations step by step, you need to understand exactly what you are trying to do. A reconciliation is done after recording the month's financial business in the journal. Think about what you did with the journal's cash column. Starting with the first of the month's checking account balance, you added the deposits and subtracted the checks. The cash column acts like a checkbook; the month's end cash column total is what you think you have in the bank at month's end.

The bank also has an idea of what you have because they keep track of your deposits and checks. Because the journal and the bank are keeping track of the same money, they should have close to the same amount. Mistakes on your behalf or the bank's will cause differences. There will also be a difference if the bank records something you have not recorded, such as service charges, interest payments, or returned checks. Also, if you have written checks or made deposits that have not yet made it through the banking system, there will be a difference.

Your focus is on reconciling the journal to the bank. Use the journal, not the checkbook. Since the journal entries are taken from the checkbook, they should be the same. But if you use the checkbook, you will miss any errors you make in the journal. So the journal is what you must reconcile.

A Step-by-Step Guide

Here is an orderly guide to reconciling a bank account:
1. Clear off your work area. When you are working with checks, journals, and statements, the last thing you need is a clutter of receipts or church newsletters.
2. Place the journal, an adding machine, a pad, a sharp pencil, and this month's bank statement (see page 145) on your desk. You also need last month's bank reconciliation (see page 146). If this is the first month since you opened the account, you, of course, would not have last month's statement. If this is so, ignore the steps that refer to last month's reconciliation. If you have not reconciled the bank in the past, the section after this step-by-step guide relates what to do.
3. Tell spouse, kids, coworkers—anyone within earshot— "Don't bother me, I'm doing a *bank reconciliation!*"
4. Pray. Ask God to give you wisdom, peace, and ample patience as you do this service for him.
5. Tear open the end of the bank statement envelope. Tearing open the end saves the envelope as a handy pouch for old checks when you are done.
6. The envelope includes a bank statement, canceled checks, and perhaps some old deposit slips and "mystery" slips. Mystery slips are such things as returned check notices or interbank transfer notices. Sort the

Pleasant Valley Bank
Bank Statement
June 30, 1986

Pleasant Valley Community Church
1179 Johnson Road
Pleasant Valley, NC 29401

Beginning balance	Deposits & interest	Checks	Service charge	Ending balance
18,796.68	5,208.82	2,362.08	9.85	21,633.57

Deposits:

6/1	1,231.80
6/8	1,591.91
6/15	1,000.21
6/22	1,286.30

Checks:

6/1	380.60, 111.90
6/3	100.11
6/5	38.96, 40.00
6/6	100.00, 673.40
6/7	198.60, NSF 100.00
6/16	119.91, Draft 198.60
6/18	300.00

Interest Earnings $98.60

bank statement, the old deposit slips, the old checks, and the mystery slips into stacks.

7. On the top of that paper write the church name and date and the words "Bank Reconciliation."

8. On the next line write "Balance per bank." Look on the bank statement to find the *ending* balance and write it down. You are now ready to look for things that explain why the bank balance is not the same as your journal's cash column.

9. Find any deposits that the bank does not show on the bank statement. These are the ones that were made after the cut-off day for the bank statement. If you made a

National 45-104 Eye-Ease 45-404 20/20 Buff Made in USA

Pleasant Valley Community Church
Bank Reconciliation
June 1986

		1	2	3	4
Balance per bank			2163357		
Deposits in transit			161059		
Outstanding Checks					
308 5/15/86		1000			
322 6/30/86		25096			
323 6/30/86		148631			
324 6/30/86		123299			
325 6/30/86		19631			
			317657		
Balance per Journal			2006769		
Proof of Deposits					
Deposits per bank		520882			
− Interest		− 9860			
− May's Deposit in Transit		− 23180			
+ June's Deposit in Transit		161059			
June's Deposits per Journal		548901			

deposit that the bank has not yet recorded, write the amount under the bank balance on your bank reconciliation and label it "Deposits in transit." Since these are deposits the bank does not yet know about, add them to the balance per bank.

10. You are now ready to prove your deposits. Receipts given to donors should equal the deposits. This proves the deposits:

Bank deposits
Minus deposits in transit at end of last month
Plus deposits in transit at the end of this month
Minus any interest earned

The month's deposits in the journal

Your answer should be the total deposits recorded in the journal. Use only the total for the deposits recorded in the journal. Do not use the total that includes the beginning cash balance. If the answer does not equal the deposits recorded in the journal, do these things to hunt for your error:

a. Redo the calculation.
b. Add the members' receipts. Make sure that the total matches the total in the journal. If not, find the mistake and correct.
c. Check the addition on the members' receipts.
d. Add the total for the weeks and trace them back to the deposits made for that week.

This process should locate the error. After you have proved your deposits, you are ready to work on the checks.

11. Put the checks returned in the bank statement in check number order. Trace the checks back to last month's outstanding checks and to the journal. Put check marks in the journal beside the checks that cleared the bank. You are looking for two things. First, you are trying to find the checks that have not cleared the bank. After you find them all, add them up and subtract the total from

the bank balance.

The second thing you are looking for is errors in your journal. These happen when you incorrectly record a check or when you do not record a check at all. When you find these errors, correct them in the journal and change everything affected by the error, including the amounts in the fund columns and the column totals.

At this point you will have a bank balance with deposits in transit added and outstanding checks subtracted. These are all your balance per bank adjustments unless you find a bank error. Everything else changes your balance per journal.

12. Record the items included on the mystery slips in the journal. If the slip is a draft, record it just like a check. If it is a bad check from a donor, record it as a negative deposit: reduce the cash column and the fund columns the gift first went into.

13. Record the service charge in the journal just like a check.

At this point, the reconciled balance should equal the cash column total in the journal. If not, you have a problem. You have already learned how to prove the deposits. If the proof works, there is not an error in the deposit's portion of the reconciliation. It is in the check half. If this is so, carefully rework steps thirteen through fifteen. Also check the adding of the journal checks section. Remember James 1:2: "Consider it pure joy, my brothers, whenever you face trials of many kinds."

When you are done, you will have a bank reconciliation that equals the journal's cash column.

Estimating the Beginning Balance

If in the past the church did not balance the account, you must estimate a balance. First, find the latest bank statement. Review the checkbook for the last few deposits. Find any that the bank statement does not have. Then look at the last few months' checks and compare these to the checks that show up on the bank statements. Try to find all the checks that are not on a bank statement.

Now arrive at a balance: take the final bank statement account balance and add any deposits that do not show on the bank statement and subtract any checks that have been written but are not on the bank statement. This is your cash balance. If you painstakingly search for deposits and outstanding checks, you will have the best guess of your checking account balance. If you estimate the bank balance at the first of the month, you can use the work later as if it were last month's bank reconciliation.

APPENDIX 3
SAMPLE BUDGET

This appendix shows the 1988 budget for First (Scots) Presbyterian Church in Charleston, South Carolina. Many thanks to the congregation and the session for sharing this.

FIRST (SCOTS) PRESBYTERIAN CHURCH
Budget for 1988
Receipts

	Budget 1987	Budget 1988
Pledges	*$445,568	**$476,687
Anticipated New Pledges and Non-pledged Contributions	37,250	37,250
Presbytery Support for Campus Ministry	0	0
Loose Offerings	12,500	12,500
Church School	1,000	1,000
Rentals	3,500	3,500
Ministers' Benevolence Fund	1,500	1,500
Miscellaneous	1,500	1,500
Subtotal	$502,818	$533,937
Anticipated pledges of members who pledged in 1987 that have not yet pledged for 1988		20,263
Total estimated receipts	$502,818	$554,200

*As of 3/1/87.   **As of 1/12/88.

Budget

	1986 Budget	1987 Budget	1988 Challenge Budget
A. Benevolences:			
1. Presbytery	$71,610	$76,000	$80,270
2. Direct Missionary Support	4,000	4,000	4,000
3. Presbytery Office Support	6,387	7,000	8,000
4. Montreat Capital Campaign			1,000
5. Hilton Head Conference Center			4.000
Total Benevolences	$81,997	$87,000	$97,270
B. Witness Division:			
1. TV Outreach	$25,000	$25,000	$25,000
2. Outreach	2,500	2,500	
a. World Mission Expense			1,000
b. Faith Development			600
c. New Member			400
d. Summer Projects			250
e. Miscellaneous			250
Total Witness	$27,500	$27,500	$27,500
C. Campus Ministry			
1. Campus Ministry	$2,700	$500	$1,800
D. Christian Service			
1. CICM	$6,000	$6,000	$9,440
2. Meals on Wheels	650	1,200	2,600
3. Other Local Missions:			
a. Hospice	1,000	1,000	1,000
b. Florence Critt	500	500	500
c. Soup Kitchen	1,000	1,000	In CICM
d. Habitat for Humanity	500	500	600
e. Help	350	350	400
Total Christian Service	$10,000	$10,550	$14,540
E. Worship:			
1. Music Program:			
a. Salaries	$27,712	$22,680	
(1) Music Director & Organist			$22,260
(2) Other Sal. & Fees			8,810
b. Activities & Supplies	7,400	11,100	2,600
c. Maintenance	4,550	2,800	4,170
d. Continuing Education			700
2. Sanc. Supplies & Flowers	1,500	1,500	1,500

	1986 Budget	1987 Budget	1988 Challenge Budget
3. Visiting Ministers	400	600	600
4. Scottish Heritage Sunday	500	500	500
5. Newspaper Ads	2,200	3,025	3,025
6. Bulletin Printing	In Office Sup.	12,000	12,000
Total Worship	$44,262	$54,205	$56,165
F. Christian Education:			
1. Curriculum and Supplies	$5,270	$6,000	$6,000
2. Youth Fellowship	2,100	2,000	6,450
3. Leadership Training	1,560	1,900	2,400
4. Nursery Salaries	2,250	5,360	6,000
5. Nursery Supplies			800
6. Library/Audio Visual Aids			1,500
7. Miscellaneous	404	1,000	250
8. Survey	2,404	2,404	3,685
9. These Days	330	250	282
10. Recreation	0	600	600
11. Vacation Bible School	0	1,000	1,200
Total Christian Ed.	$14,318	$20,514	$29,167
G. Fellowship:			
1. Activities	$0	$700	$1,500
2. Kitchen Supplies	1,500	1,500	1,500
3. Kitchen Labor	4,500	1,000	1,000
4. Kitchen Food	0	3,672	2,500
5. Kitchen Manager			5,200
Total Fellowship	$6,000	$6,872	$11,700
H. Business Administration:			
1. Churchwide Support:			
a. Office Sup/Postage	$14,000	$14,000	$13,045
b. Telephone	6,000	6,500	7,210
c. Office F&E Purchases	6,700	8,000	7,570
d. Office F&E Maintenance	0	5,000	4,320
e. Personnel Insurance	13,715	6,056	8,965
f. FICA	10,500	6,293	7,625
g. Continuing Education	1,500	1,500	1,000
2. Internal Office:			
a. Salaries	49,755	41,100	43,570
b. Misc (T-Sup;Audit)	1,300	1,300	1,010
3. Minister's Disc. Fund	500	500	500
Total Business Adm.	$103,970	$90,249	$94,815

	1986 Budget	1987 Budget	1988 Challenge Budget
I. Church Bldg. & Grounds:			
1. Bldg. Maintenance	$12,000	$12,000	$4,500
2. Grounds Maintenance	4,000	4,000	2,400
3. Utilities	16,000	18,000	17,235
4. Mech. Equipment Maint.	2,000	600	1,735
5. Mech. Equipment Purchase		1,200	1,200
6. Sexton/Maid/Grds Salary	16,091	18,000	26,960
7. Sexton Supplies	2,400	1,000	1,390
8. Insurance	9,000	10,000	13,000
Total Bldg. & Grounds	$61,491	$64,800	$68,420
J. Minister & Assoc. Min.:			
1. Salary, Allow., Ann.	$114,783		
a. Senior Minister		$57,200	
(1) Salary			$39,590
(2) Housing Allowance			$12,840
(3) Utilities			4,200
(4) Car Allowance			4,000
b. Assoc. Minister		28,100	
(1) Salary			$17,655
(2) Housing Allowance			$6,420
(3) Utilities			2,800
(4) Car Allowance			2,800
c. Assoc. for Christian Ed.		26,500	
(1) Salary			$17,143
(2) Housing Allowance			$6,420
(3) Utilities			2,800
(4) Car Allowance			2,800
d. FICA		5,707	6,283
e. Annuities		13,416	14,193
f. Insurance		8,944	10,724
g. Continuing Education	1,800	1,800	2,100
Total Ministers	$116,583	$141,667	$152,768
Grand Total	$468,821	$503,857	$554,145

APPENDIX 4
TAX FORMS

Below are the tax forms talked about in chapter 11.

Tax Tables

Use the tax tables to look up the amount to withhold. A complete set is in the IRS's *Circular E.*

MARRIED Persons–**SEMIMONTHLY** Payroll Period
(For Wages Paid After December 1988)

And the wages are—		And the number of withholding allowances claimed is—										
At least	But less than	0	1	2	3	4	5	6	7	8	9	10
		The amount of income tax to be withheld shall be—										
$0	$135	$0	$0	$0	$0	$0	$0	$0	$0	$0	$0	$0
135	140	1	0	0	0	0	0	0	0	0	0	0
140	145	1	0	0	0	0	0	0	0	0	0	0
145	150	2	0	0	0	0	0	0	0	0	0	0
150	155	3	0	0	0	0	0	0	0	0	0	0
155	160	4	0	0	0	0	0	0	0	0	0	0
160	165	4	0	0	0	0	0	0	0	0	0	0
165	170	5	0	0	0	0	0	0	0	0	0	0
170	175	6	0	0	0	0	0	0	0	0	0	0
175	180	7	0	0	0	0	0	0	0	0	0	0
180	185	7	0	0	0	0	0	0	0	0	0	0
185	190	8	0	0	0	0	0	0	0	0	0	0
190	195	9	0	0	0	0	0	0	0	0	0	0
195	200	10	0	0	0	0	0	0	0	0	0	0
200	205	10	0	0	0	0	0	0	0	0	0	0
205	210	11	0	0	0	0	0	0	0	0	0	0
210	215	12	0	0	0	0	0	0	0	0	0	0

Form 941

Form 941 must be filed at the end of every quarter. It shows the amount that you withheld and the social security taxes due.

Form **941**	**Employer's Quarterly Federal Tax Return**			
(Rev. January 1989) Department of the Treasury Internal Revenue Service	4141 ► For Paperwork Reduction Act Notice, see page 2. **Please type or print.**			

Type or print your name, address, employer identification number, and calendar quarter of return as shown on original. ►

Name (as distinguished from trade name) **Summerville Community Church**   Date quarter ended **12-31**

Trade name, if any

Employer identification number **57-9816611**

Address and ZIP code **1350 Roddington   Summerville AN 21109**

YOUR COPY

If you do not have to file returns in the future, check here . . . ► ☑   Date final wages paid . . . ►

If you are a seasonal employer, see **Seasonal employer** on page 2 and check here . . . ►☐

1a	Number of employees (except household) employed in the pay period that includes March 12th ►	1a	2
b	If you are a subsidiary corporation AND your parent corporation files a consolidated Form 1120, enter parent corporation employer identification number (EIN) . . ► 1b		
2	Total wages and tips subject to withholding, plus other compensation . . . . ►	2	4062 —
3	Total income tax withheld from wages, tips, pensions, annuities, sick pay, gambling, etc. . . .	3	220 —
4	Adjustment of withheld income tax for preceding quarters of calendar year (see instructions) .	4	
5	Adjusted total of income tax withheld (see instructions)	5	220 —
6	Taxable social security wages paid . . . . $ 4062 × 15.02% (.1502) . .	6	610 13
7a	Taxable tips reported . . . . $ × 15.02% (.1502) .	7a	
b	Taxable hospital insurance wages paid . . . $ × 2.9% (.029). .	7b	
8	Total social security taxes (add lines 6, 7a, and 7b)	8	610 13
9	Adjustment of social security taxes (see instructions for required explanation)	9	
10	Adjusted total of social security taxes (see instructions) . . . . ►	10	610 13
11	Backup withholding (see instructions)	11	
12	Adjustment of backup withholding tax for preceding quarters of calendar year . . . . . ►	12	
13	Adjusted total of backup withholding	13	
14	Total taxes (add lines 5, 10, and 13)	14	830 13
15	Advance earned income credit (EIC) payments, if any	15	
16	Net taxes (subtract line 15 from line 14). **This must equal line IV below** (plus line IV of Schedule A (Form 941) if you have treated backup withholding as a separate liability)	16	830 13
17	Total deposits for quarter, including overpayment applied from a prior quarter, from your records . ►	17	830 13
18	Balance due (subtract line 17 from line 16). This should be less than $500. Pay to IRS . . . ►	18	-0-
19	If line 17 is more than line 16, enter overpayment here ► $ and check if to be: ☐ Applied to next return **OR** ☐ Refunded.		

Record of Federal Tax Liability (Complete if line 16 is $500 or more.) See the instructions on page 4 for details before checking these boxes.
Check only if you made eighth-monthly deposits using the 95% rule ► ☐   Check only if you are a first time 3-banking-day depositor ► ☐

Show tax liability here, **not deposits**. IRS gets deposit data from FTD coupons.

Date wages paid		First month of quarter		Second month of quarter		Third month of quarter
1st through 3rd	A		I		Q	
4th through 7th	B		J		R	
8th through 11th	C		K		S	
12th through 15th	D	138.35	L	138.35	T	138.35
16th through 19th	E		M		U	
20th through 22nd	F		N		V	
23rd through 25th	G		O		W	
26th through the last	H	138.36	P	138.36	X	138.36
Total liability for month	I	276.71	II	276.71	III	276.71

(left margin: Do NOT Show Federal Tax Deposits Here)

IV Total for quarter (add lines *I*, *II*, and *III*). **This must equal line 16 above** . . . . ► 830 13

Sign Here   Under penalties of perjury, I declare that I have examined this return, including accompanying schedules and statements, and to the best of my knowledge and belief, it is true, correct, and complete.

Signature ► **Pastor Jim James**   Title ► **Pastor**   Date ► **Jan 18,**

Form W-4

Form W-4 is completed by the employee on the first work day. The church keeps this form to refer to when determining the amount to withhold.

Form 8109

Give Form 8109 to the bank when you are making a tax deposit.

Form W-2

Complete Form W-2 after the year ends. It recaps all of an employee's information.

1 Control number 22222	For Paperwork Reduction Act Notice, see separate instructions OMB No. 1545-0008	For Official Use Only ▶	
2 Employer's name, address, and ZIP code Summerville Community church 1350 Roddington Summerville AN 21109	3 Employer's identification number 57-9816611	4 Employer's state I.D. number	

5 Statutory employee / Deceased / Pension plan / Legal rep. / 942 emp. / Subtotal / Deferred compensation / Void

6 Allocated tips | 7 Advance EIC payment

8 Employee's social security number 241-16-1111	9 Federal income tax withheld 440	10 Wages, tips, other compensation 8124	11 Social security tax withheld 609
12 Employee's name (first, middle, last) IRA Smith 15 Stout St Summerville AN. 21109	13 Social security wages 8124	14 Social security tips	

16 (See Instr. for Forms W-2/W-2P) | 16a Fringe benefits incl. in Box 10

15 Employee's address and ZIP code | 17 State income tax | 18 State wages, tips, etc. | 19 Name of state

20 Local income tax | 21 Local wages, tips, etc. | 22 Name of locality

Form W-2 Wage and Tax Statement **1989** · Copy A For Social Security Administration · Dept. of the Treasury—IRS

Form W-3

Send in Form W-3 with all the church employees' W-2 forms.

DO NOT STAPLE

1 Control number 33333	For Official Use Only ▶ OMB No. 1545-0008		3	4	5 Number of statements attached
Kind of Payer ▶	2 941/941E ✓ Military CT-1 942 943 Medicare gov't. emp.				
6 Allocated tips	7 Advance EIC payments		8		
9 Federal income tax withheld 880	10 Wages, tips, and other compensation 16248		11 Social security tax withheld 1220		
12 Employer's state I.D. number 57-9816611	13 Social security wages 16248		14 Social security tips -0-		
15 Employer's identification number 57 — 9816611			16 Establishment number		
17 Employer's name Summerville Community church 1350 Roddington Summerville AN 21109			18 Gross annuity, pension, etc. (Form W-2P)		
			20 Taxable amount (Form W-2P)		
19 Employer's address and ZIP code (If available, place label over boxes 15, 17, and 19.)			21 Income tax withheld by third-party payer		

Under penalties of perjury, I declare that I have examined this return and accompanying documents, and to the best of my knowledge and belief they are true, correct, and complete. In the case of documents without recipients' identifying numbers, I have complied with the requirements of the law in attempting to secure such numbers from the recipients.

Signature ▶ Pastor Jim James Title ▶ Pastor Date ▶ Jan 30

Form W-3 Transmittal of Income and Tax Statements **1988** · Department of the Treasury Internal Revenue Service